Lacan Today

Lacan Today

OCLC Record

Psychoanalysis, Science, Religion

Alexandre Leupin

OTHER

Other Press
New York

Production Editor: Robert D. Hack

This book was set in 11pt Goudy by Alpha Graphics of Pittsfield, NH.

10 9 8 7 6 5 4 3 2 1

Library of Congress Cataloging-in-Publication Data

Leupin, Alexandre, 1948–
  Lacan today : psychoanalysis, science, religion / by Alexandre Leupin.
    p. cm.
Includes bibliographical references and index.
  ISBN 1-892746-90-5 (pbk. : alk. paper)
  1. Lacan, Jacques, 1901– I. Title.
  BF109.L28 L48 2004
  150.19'5'092–dc22

                                                    2003022932

To Jeff Humphries

Teaching must submit common notions to the grinder.

Jacques Lacan, *Écrits*, p. 836

Contents

Acknowledgments

My deepest gratitude goes to my wife Kate, who spent countless hours to put this book into real English, and to Dr. Amadou Guissé, whose mathematical competence proved invaluable. I also wish to thank Judith Feher-Gurewich for her enthusiasm and support for this project. The book's redaction benefited from a research leave that Louisiana State University generously granted to me during the 2001 fall semester, as well as from a visiting professorship at the Université de Poitiers, France, during the summer of 2002.

Introduction

Meaning occurs only when a discourse is translated into another discourse.
("*L'étourdit*," *Autres écrits*, p. 480)

If the unconscious exists, then Lacan is the only twentieth-century thinker who has drawn the consequences of Freud's discovery to their ultimate limits. I propose here what some will take as bombastic hyperbole: Lacan's radical reevaluation of human thinking is comparable to Einstein's. However, since Lacan's contribution plays itself out in the interstices between the humanities and hard science, an unusual space to occupy, it runs the risk of being neglected by thinkers belonging to either field.

Though Lacan's thought is making tremendous inroads in countries of Latin culture, in the Anglophone sphere it is slowly fading from public awareness. Often Lacan has been nothing more than a pawn in the bundling together of contradictory doctrines labeled as "French thought," or has been reduced to a kind of ghetto presence—a means of exchange between psychoanalysts or specialists in the humanities.

My contention is that what Lacan said and wrote is of interest to a large public, and that his consignment to oblivion is reversible: my book will have no other aim than to demonstrate that Lacan's thinking has

vast implications, not only for college professors or practicing psychoanalysts but also for scientists, epistemologists, and, yes, the common
man and woman.

At first glance, it can be said that Lacan is a specialist in the for-
mations of the unconscious. Hence, his discourse is primarily addressed
to a relatively small number of other specialists, such as psychoanalysts
interested in the theoretical aspects of their profession.

However, like Freud before him, Lacan deals with sex and culture,
science and philosophy: his works encompasses topics bound to interest a larger public. This interest is not simply the consequence of Freud's
or Lacan's vast culture. It has to do with the universal effects of their
thought; once the existence of the unconscious is admitted, then no
field of human activity remains unaffected: "The psychoanalytic experience demonstrates nothing other than that none of our acts are out
of the unconscious' purview."[1] Science (and the consequences to humankind of its expansion), humanities, philosophy, literature, mythology,
and religion all can be submitted to a psychoanalytic rereading.

Also, since Lacan has produced a general epistemology that over-
comes the opposition between the humanities and hard sciences, his work
has implications that go far beyond academia and psychoanalysis. In the
Anglophone world, though, the interest in Lacan has been limited either
to some professional psychoanalytical circles, or, at the other end of the
spectrum, to a small academic elite, usually comprised of humanists, with
no direct experience in psychoanalysis and little interest in the scientific
and epistemological questions Lacan's work tackles.

But there are other reasons for the marginalization of Lacan's work,
and they are numerous; we can distinguish here between internal causes,
such as those depending on Lacan himself, and external factors, misunderstandings stemming from the way the works insert themselves in
a particular context.[2]

---

1. *Écrits*; Paris: Le Seuil, 1966, p. 514.
2. For an overview of these crisscrossed misunderstandings, see the excellent
contributions collected by Judith Feher-Gurewich and Michel Tort, *Lacan and the New
Wave in American Psychonanalysis*; New York: Other Press, 1999, and by Jean-Michel
Rabaté, *Lacan in America*; New York: Other Press, 2000.

The primary internal cause of misunderstanding, in my opinion, resides in Lacan's style, which defies clear translation;[3] his writing very often falls (on purpose) into a Mallarméan mannerism, the high and obscure style practiced by French doctors around the 1930s. On the other hand, if the *Seminars*, which are a reworked transcription of his oral teaching, appear more easily accessible, it is the result of Jacques-Alain Miller's work. His enormous effort in publishing his version of the transcription has been concerned with replacing the accent of Lacan's own, now vanished voice by emphasizing the logical underpinnings of the *Seminars*. All the signifying effects once carried by Lacan's voice, gestures, and body—reticences, emphases, silence, ironies that made his living discourse clear—have been substituted by the logical coherence of writing. Let me make clear that this solution, the one chosen by Miller, was one of the few possible options; one need only consult the pirated transcripts of the *Seminars* to understand how confusing a literally faithful reproduction would have been.

Another wall between Lacan and an Anglophone public was erected by Lacan himself. I am talking about Lacan's anti-Americanism, which is much broader than his attacks against ego psychology or his criticism of Freud's heirs who emigrated to the United States following the rise of Hitler. The critique of the American way of life is in fact a critique of the accent given to the imaginary ego in American psychotherapy; for Lacan, the American psychology of his times is something akin to a religious belief, through which egos alienate themselves by letting the forces of an economic market define them: "The ego is the theology of free enterprise."[4] His criticism of ego psychology is at the same time a repudiation of the American idea of possessing a way to happiness: "The practice of psychoanalysis in the American sphere of influence has been downgraded to a means of obtaining 'success' and to a mode of request for 'happiness': it is a repudiation of

---

3. On the problem of translating Lacan, see the essay by Dennis Porter, "Psychoanalysis and the Task of the Translator," in *Lacan and the Human Sciences*, Alexandre Leupin, ed.; Lincoln: University of Nebraska Press, 1991.

4. *Écrits*, p. 335. See also the cliché of the "cultural anhistorism of the United States of North America," p. 402.

psychoanalysis."[5] In Lacan's view, which has a lot to do with his own imaginary, the United States stands as the antithesis of psychoanalysis. He contests the undeniable success of American society because he reads it through Old World lenses; between the supremacy of the Symbolic order (which is not modifiable by individual will) and the unconscious (which, by definition, also escapes modification by individuals), Lacan defines a very narrow path for the ego, whose freedom of action is constrained by the two poles that crush it: the controls of the Symbolic order and the uncontrollable obscurity of the unconscious. Very little space is left for the exercise of free will, despite the social dynamics of American society (for example), whose credos are change and belief in progress and where individual freedom is paramount. All the accomplishments brought about by the constant reinvention of the American ego are therefore denounced as illusory by Lacan; what an American may consider to be progress is for him a deeper and deeper alienation. This haughty repudiation, by which the very success of a society is morally condemned because it doesn't fit the theory, has done nothing to endear Lacan to Americans. We may read the repudiation of ego psychology as a stern refusal of American civilization in toto by Lacan. The pragmatic success of this culture counts for nothing in an Old World vision that privileges conceptual coherence and theoretical constructs over practical solutions.

Another major obstacle (and certainly not only in America) to understanding Lacan's work is a firm belief, by both the public and psychologists, in the "consistency" of the ego. As some of my students say, echoing Popeye, when I introduce them to psychoanalysis: "I know who I am and what I want." No evidence of the existence of a structure beyond the self, such as the social dimension of language, no inkling about another, unconscious stage where desire deploys its effects, no pointing to a hidden identity will shake this faith in the solidity of self-consciousness, and any devaluation of this belief will be met by denial.

---

5. *Écrits*, p. 416. See also the caricature at pp. 590–591: "A team of egos less equal than autonomous offers itself to Americans to guide them towards happiness, without disturbing the autonomies (egoistical or not) which pave the road with their conflictless spheres, so that the American way reaches happiness." A Constitution, like that of the United States, that prescribes a right to happiness is of course anathema to a Lacanian way of thinking.

The fact that Lacan puts the ego under siege is not welcome in these quarters. The idea that our ego and our consciousness are submitted to an unconscious determination about which very little can be done is repellent to most people. Moreover, this belief in the freedom of the ego is not easily dismissed because we are surrounded by the evidence of its consequences, in the form of a much freer and much more dynamic society; and so, from the start, Lacan's pessimism is thought to be invalidated by the belief in the boundless possibilities of the future and the real results of American optimism. The pragmatic success of the United States leaves little space for discussion of theoretical or other constraints and creates a reluctance to relinquish the very belief in this success and substitute it with an unconscious structure that renounces our liberty. However, a close look at this structure should not be rejected, if only to make the meaning of our freedom clearer.

Thirdly, and linked to the very success of this pragmatism, one must recognize that there is a widespread reluctance in the public sphere toward acceptance of a doctrinaire discourse such as Lacan's (I emphasize the difference here between doctrinaire, meaning revisable when necessary, and dogmatic, which is not subject to revision); the general public has little taste for a discourse built and developed through rigorous principles. Common sense always leans toward pragmatism, not systematic theory, toward anecdotal and empirical evidence, not logical proof, toward feelings, not arguments. Doctrine is confused with dogmatism and felt as restrictive and oppressive; on the contrary, it should be viewed as liberating—from false ideas, for example. Any thought comprises some amount of doctrine, and especially thought that claims to be nondoctrinaire.

However there is a caveat, as Lacan writes: "Our function (as psychoanalysts) has nothing doctrinaire. We do not have to answer to any ultimate truth, especially neither for nor against any religion."[6] That is, the doctrinal will stop just before it reaches truth (it cannot go further), and this truth will always be the singular truth of an individual, not an overarching transcendence. In other words, applied psychoanalysis, which deals through the cure with the patient's singularity, is the place where the theoretical construct leaves space open for practical considerations; Lacan himself emphasized that you need not be

---

6. *Écrits*, p. 818.

a Lacanian in order to be a good pyschoanalyst; conversely, not all Lacanians, however familiar they may be with the theory, will be good psychoanalysts.

A coherent doctrine is, however, indispensable in order to deal with questions about truth, desire, and sexuality without falling into subjectivity and impressionism; if a statement has some general validity, then it cannot be considered a mere opinion.

A fourth obstacle to the acceptance of Lacan's work consists in the circumstances surrounding the performative aspect of his thought; whatever he wrote or said, it was always addressed to a specific group of listeners or readers (psychoanalysts, students in philosophy, academics, the anonymous and silent gaze of the *Seminars'* public, the general public, anonymous as well, of the *Écrits*, and so on). For example, he introduces the *Écrits* thus: "We want to lead the reader to a consequence where he has to furnish his own effort when he reads these writings, which mark the course and whose style is *formulated according to their address*."[7] Or, on the preceding page: "Style is the person to whom I address myself." Indeed, when you write or speak, you tailor your style to a real or imaginary addressee.

Hence, extraneous remarks, digressions, and asides abound in the works, making their understanding that much more difficult. Now that the original listeners or addressees slowly recede into history, now that Lacan has left us, we can leave these digressions aside: they add nothing to our understanding; more, they cloud the doctrinal core, which is the important matter. If there is some truth to Lacan's theories, it is not tied to the political or critical contingency of a particular historical moment, nor is it to be read through the peculiarities of a specific audience.

One may ask, Is there not only a *today* for Lacan (Is he our contemporary?), but also a *tomorrow* for him in America? The answer to that question depends on an assessment of the parts of his discourse that escape the academic drive toward obsolescence, a drive that affects psychology too.

This does not mean that Lacan is beyond criticism and that his theory possesses an ethereal eternity. It will someday be put into ques-

---

7. *Écrits*, p. 10 (my emphasis). This law, indeed, applies to any statement in the human sphere: all statements are in a sense speech acts, sent by a addresser to an addressee (be they the same individual).

tion, not according to the whims of fashion (political correctness comes immediately to mind), but by a procedure following rational rules. In the meantime, we should strive to understand him as best we can.

My bet is that Lacan can be accessible to a nonspecialized but educated public. However, in order for Lacan to reach a broader public, certain conditions have to be fully met. These conditions imply a certain turning away from Lacan's rhetoric, while at the same time remaining absolutely faithful to the essence of his thinking.

No assumptions will be made here about the reader's familiarity with psychoanalytical concepts, even if Freud has permeated everyday speech (although this popularity has taken its toll in deforming his thought beyond recognition).

Lacan warned his students very early not to be idolaters—that is, not to concede to the "tendency to use expressions that were too full of imagery."[8] On the same page, he warned about the idolatry of Freud, that is, Freud's confidence in the image as being able to render an accurate picture of the psyche. His aim, he said, was to remove this idolatry from his disciples' minds. Of course, to move away from the image not only has the effect of promoting a more rigorous and abstract discourse on the unconscious (which explains why Lacan has a certain aridity, despite the luscious language and untranslatable word play), but also ultimately offers one the chance to liberate oneself of the notion of a sacred text delivered by an all-knowing master. The same warning about idolatry applies of course to our reading of Lacan.

In particular, the only way to be faithful to Lacan's thought is to betray its expression. Lacan cannot be translated. He has to be rethought in English through and through, and basically rewritten. Hence, when I quote, all the "translations," with a few exceptions, will be mine; they will aim not at a literal fidelity—which in my opinion has been the case for almost all his translators—but at a faithful and clear rendering of the concepts. To read Lacan is to betray him—at least in regard to his style. Too often, Lacan has been translated by "biblical" exegetes who were loath to modify even a single comma from the original text. If

---

8. *Séminaire II, Le moi dans la théorie de Freud et dans la technique de la psychanalyse;* Paris: Le Seuil, 1978, p. 71.

Lacan smashes the idols, why shouldn't we be inspired by him, to the point where we will not idolize the letter of his work?

Hence, I believe that in translating Lacan we should get rid of literalism, whose results are often monstrous; Lacan's translators often sound like they are writing some English-ized French ("Englais" instead of English), an approach that runs counter to the objective of making the work more accessible. Let me give a few examples here. First, the translation of "demande" has damaging effects on both theoretical and practical levels; to render it in English as "demand"—whereas it should be translated by "request" (what we can articulate of our desire)—gives to the concept an imperious accent that it lacks in French. Another crucial example of mistranslation concerns the famous "Il n'y a pas de rapport sexuel." To translate this as "There is no sexual relationship" leads to a complete misunderstanding about what Lacan means: "rapport" here does not concern coitus, but designates a logical and symbolic relation. Hence, through the mistranslation as "sexual relationships," the problem of gendering is envisioned at the empirical level and the whole purpose of the Lacanian conceptual edifice collapses.

Also, how do you go about translating "~~LA~~ femme n'existe pas"? In French and in the context of Lacanian thought, it means that an essence of woman is not reachable through language and representation, that no general class of ideas can be construed that would accurately reflect femininity; only one translation is possible: "Women don't exist," meaning that women have to be taken one by one. Similarly, if Lacan in a schema indicates this nonexistence of a class of women by barring the French "~~LA~~" the equivalent rendering in English should be a barred "~~Women~~."

The idolatry of the signifier manifested by some translators also runs counter to Lacan's efforts toward inscribing psychoanalysis in the realm of modernity. In magic, rituals, and religion there are sacred traditions and texts where such a literal respect may be warranted, but the text of our times is constantly rewritten and revised to accommodate the truths it was not able to foresee. As Newton rewrote Galileo, and Einstein Newton (to the point of the newcomer sometimes erasing his predecessor's contribution), Lacan rewrote Freud, and the time has already come where people are rewriting Lacan, witness for example Judith Feher-Gurewich's work or Alain Badiou's criticism of Lacan's use of infinitude.[9] Nevertheless, the constant revision imposed by modernity is possible only if what has to be revised is clearly grasped and if the revisionism is based on a rational basis. I could say that my only ambition, which in my opinion has been only partially accomplished up to now, is to translate Lacan *in English*.

To assume that a clearly delineated doctrinal core exists means that something of Lacan, and this also applies to Freud in German, is exact or true (or both) and thus escapes the local constraints ("Frenchness," address to a specific public, misreading of or by America) through which his thought is expressed. In other words, *something* of Lacan is transmissible in another language, something is *translatable*.

We should stress here that the translation problem is not specific to a transfer of meaning between two languages; from the outset, a French reader is also forced by Lacan himself to retranslate the work in order to explain it actively. The works are not an object of culture, something that would present the reader with ideas he has already understood, and which would make him the object of a passive reading; Lacan passionately asks for an active reader, engaged himself in the construction of a theory, for which the reader has to "furnish his own effort."[10] In this respect, a French reader is no more privileged than an Anglophone one, and maybe even less so, since a Francophone may easily fall in the trap of too quick an understanding. Suffice it to say I do not fantasize a hyper-brilliant audience on one side of the Atlantic and a dumb one on the other. The problem has been, in both cases (and with notable exceptions), with the way Lacan has been transmitted to his readers, be it through translation or explanation. Specifically, writing this book has meant for me a double translation: first, displacing Lacan's style to mine (admittedly more pedestrian), then translating the result in English.

In fact, a model for reading Lacan is none other than his reading of Freud. Beyond the now trivial "return to Freud" lies a paradigm for an interpretation of Lacan, if we turn on him the interpretation he applied to the master. First of all, for Lacan, the Freudian corpus is not a

---

9. See Alain Badiou, "Sujet et infini," in *Conditions*; Paris: Le Seuil, 1992.
10. *Écrits*, p. 10.

Bible; since Freud strives to inscribe psychoanalysis in the realm of modern science, his writings are (like scientific theories) susceptible to a constant revision—hence, for example, the rejection of Freud's reliance on biology by Lacan.

However, that doesn't mean that the essential points of Freud's discovery should be systematically contested, for example on ideological grounds. A lot of so-called criticism today is falsely lucid: it basically confuses critical thinking with being negative, it distorts works, sometimes not even purposefully, but by virtue of sheer misunderstanding, it promotes a particular, often political point of view, and it cuts thinking off from its broader underpinnings. In brief, critical thinking today is increasingly subject to misunderstanding, distortion, and sheer falsity; denigration and resentment often pass for criticism. To take only one example, you are not automatically a phallocrat because you speak about the phallus.

In the "*Séminaire de Caracas*,"[11] Lacan summed up his relationship to Freud in a paradoxical fashion: "You can be Lacanians, if you want. As far as I am concerned, I am Freudian." The first part gives an essential liberty to the follower(s); you may be a Lacanian, if you wish to be so—we are very far, here, from the image of a ferocious and dictatorial master. The second part reaffirms the fidelity to Freud's teaching, and also indicates that Lacan himself is not a Lacanian: that he doesn't believe in the (narcissistic) idolatry necessarily tied to the master of wisdom and knowledge as conceived by antiquity or Oriental philosophy.

But to be faithful to Freud, inasmuch as his doctrine can be inscribed in modern science, is the equivalent of going further than he did, and reading him in a critical manner. Therefore, the proclamation of faithfulness to Freud in "*Le séminaire de Caracas*" is immediately followed by a critique of his representation of the psyche. Lacan, again, calls into question Freud's "idolatry," specifically the imagery associated with his second topography;[12] and as far as Lacan's own contributions, which he described elsewhere as absolutely original,[13] they are reduced to the Borromean knot tying together the Real, the Symbolic, and the Imaginary: "My three agencies are not Freud's three agencies. They are

---

11. *L'Âne* 1, Avril–Mai 1981, p. 30.
12. See Chapter 1, p. 2.
13. "It has never, never been done." *Scilicet* 6–7 (1976), p. 56.

the Real, the Symbolic and the Imaginary. I ended up describing them through a topology defined by the Borromean knot."[14] At first glance, we can reduce Lacan's contribution to Freudianism to a mathematical formulation that goes against his disciples' and Freud's tendency to indulge in images, their idolatry, and the route to it can be summarized in a paradoxical way: Lacan's faithfulness to Freud produced something that goes way beyond Freud. The *"Séminaire de Caracas"* gives an excellent illustration of the mix of fidelity and distance that should be our model in reading Lacan.

Freud's contradictions are not an object of ridicule, or a cause for dismissal, but are often treated by Lacan as an impulse for further thinking; let us mention for instance, the glaring contradiction between the biological foundations of *Beyond the Pleasure Principle* and its death drive on one hand, and the symbolic, not biological, dead father of *Totem and Taboo* on the other. Freud places a biological myth and a symbolic problem side by side; Lacan, precisely by reading Freud's biologism as a myth, and then elaborating the Name-of-the-Father, restores the unity of his thought and erases the contradiction; the dialectic of symbolic forces has been reestablished through faithfulness to the core of the Freudian construction; furthermore, this faithfulness is precisely the way through which Lacan produces an advance beyond Freud.

If we can extract an interpretative model for Lacan in his reading of Freud, then of course the way Lacan maps out Freudian texts is most important. He reads Freud's works through their structure, not, again, through their imagery or their historical evolution. It means that we have to insert concepts in what I call a coherence, and then work their definitions out through their opposites and parallels: "You should refer to the notions' articulations in Freudian discourse. This is where you will notice their precise use and you will be able to recapture these notions in their new signification in order to make use of them."[15] In other words, no glossary of formal definitions will do: they freeze and isolate what are dynamic concepts, whose force can be grasped only through their contextual mapping out; the concepts have to be considered from the point of view of their respective relations.

---

14. *L'Âne* 1, Avril–Mai 1981, p. 30.

15. "Discours de Rome," *Autres écrits*, Jacques-Alain Miller, ed.; Paris: Le Seuil, 2001, p. 147.

Should we then say that Lacan is a structuralist? Although he found a lot of his inspiration in structural linguistics (Saussure) and structural anthropology (Lévi-Strauss), he went far beyond: for Lacan, the structure is a way to build a spider's web around what escapes it, the unconscious. Whereas true structuralism never was preoccupied with the point where the structure fails, one can say that this failure, which shows the structure's limit, is the object of psychoanalysis itself: where the structure falls silent, the unconscious begins: "Structuralism will last as long as symbolisms and Parnassi do: it will last as long as a literary season. . . . The structure is not closed to its own demise, because it inscribes itself in the real (the unconscious) or rather, the structure gives away, in order to give a meaning to the word 'real.'"[16]

Hence Lacan is not a structuralist *stricto sensu*, if the latter is to be characterized by a faith in the structure as a totalizing tool; for Lacan, there is something real beyond the structure, and that is the unconscious.

Nevertheless, this Lacanian emphasis on the structure explains why the reader will not be submitted here to yet another genealogy of Lacan's ideas, their origins, or the retracing of their evolution, even if this endeavor is quite useful given Lacan's allusiveness and his tendency not to quote his sources. This has been done (and well) elsewhere. Furthermore, the history of a concept doesn't shed light on the concept itself—only its articulation with surrounding ideas does. What works (according to my experience of having taught Lacan to graduate students for a number of years) is a structural apprehension of Lacan's concepts, that is, their insertion in a general coherence (which I suppose to be at work in the corpus in its entirety), their profiling in a recurrent system. My refusal to go into a history of concepts doesn't mean that no background should be evoked. But this background should remind the reader of general ideas, primary truths, not the Hegelian, Kojèvian, or Heideggerian origins of some of Lacan's concepts.

Another trap that will be avoided here is the bundling of Lacan with a vague ensemble that could be called French (or, for that matter, American) postmodernism or poststructuralism and his associa-

16. "Petit discours à l'ORTF," *Autres écrits*, p. 225. See Jean-Claude Milner, *Le périple structural*, "Lacan I," "Lacan II"; Paris: Le Seuil, 2002, pp. 141–168.

tion with such leading figures of critical theory as Paul De Man, Gilles Deleuze, Michel Foucault, and Jacques Derrida. Schematically put, Lacan has nothing to do with these schools of thought; he recognizes only one umbrella for his work and it is scientific modernity. He has to be opposed to these other thinkers inasmuch as he is a realist (in the Medieval sense of the term), whereas they are, in their majority, nominalists. Words, for Lacan, evoke something real outside of language. Quite to the contrary, nominalists (and this category encompasses most literary critics in academia and elsewhere) believe that words refer only to other words, ad infinitum. As a realist, Lacan stands as an heir to the medieval philosophical tradition and also as a follower of the scientific tradition founded by Galileo.

Furthermore, we can say of postmodernism that, from the play of the signifier and the resulting equivocality of signification, it deducts the possibility of an infinite number of possible interpretations. Lacan, while maintaining the equivocality of language, affirms to the contrary that, at least in psychoanalysis, there is only one good interpretation, and that it is absurd to pretend that all interpretations are possible.[17]

The reduplicating of Lacan's way with Freud, and its application to the corpus of Lacan himself, carries us only so far: Lacan paid infinitely more attention than did Freud to the coherence and pertinence of his methodological and epistemological models, to the point of a quasi-psychotic coherence: it is therefore much more difficult to point out discrepancies in the work. But Lacan also took his time to become Lacan, and his beginnings, while they do not anticipate the following developments, make them possible: "Our students are mistaken when they find 'already there' what our teaching has afterward discovered. Isn't it enough that what is there does not preclude what was discovered later?"[18] The theory is therefore constantly redrawn, modified, reformulated, but very rarely put in contradiction with itself; the movement of Lacan's thinking is more an expansion and redirection than an outright rejection of the antecedents. As Jean-Claude Milner has shown in *L'oeuvre claire*, the models change over time, the doctrinal

---

17. See in particular *Séminaire XI, Les quatre concepts fondamentaux de la psychoanalyse*; Paris: Le Seuil, 1973, pp. 224–226.

18. *Écrits*, p. 67.

core is constantly redrawn, but its coherence is maintained. What permits this evolving coherence is an early choice by Lacan, a choice that is at the same time pedagogic and conceptual: the reference that will formalize psychoanalysis will be modern logic and mathematics. As early as 1953, in "Function and Field of Speech and Language,"[19] Lacan refers to a topological model—and this in a nonmetaphorical way, contrary to what would be the habit among humanists. From then on, the mathematical model will never be far away in his works; it will give Lacan an unparalleled coherence when he explores the intersection between the humanities and science.

One of Freud's ambiguities that Lacan erases without hesitation is the question concerning the object of psychoanalysis. This is an essential step, since psychoanalysis's claim to scientificity rests on its ability to circumscribe a specific object, without which there is no science. Reading Freud, we get the impression that this object of psychoanalysis is sometimes the body, its biology, its dynamics, sometimes the mind and its contradictions, sometimes the brain and its functioning. There is no such uncertainty in Lacan: the sole object of psychoanalysis is the symbolic effect of language on the mind; that is why the contributions of psychoanalysis to physiology not only are nil, but *should be* nil: "The object of psychoanalysis is not man, it is what he lacks. This is not an absolute lack, but the lack of an object."[20]

By putting the emphasis on language, Lacan defines the object of psychoanalysis as first and foremost a signifier. This was only implicit in Freud, but it helps restore psychoanalysis's coherence and take Freud's "*Id* thinks" (there is a thinking process that is not conscious) to its ultimate consequences. In particular, there is no thinking without words; Lacan here makes a definitive break with the conception Greek antiquity had of a soul (*anima*) deprived of language and preexisting its expression in a discourse. If the objects of psychoanalysis are signifiers, then the "unconscious is structured like a language" and the means of inquiry have to be adapted to this linguistic object.

This stance doesn't preclude the benefit of any advances in neurology and the physiology of the brain. What it excludes is the transference of natural processes to a realm that is separated from them; human ca-

---

19. *Écrits*, pp. 320–321.
20. "Réponses à des étudiants en philosophie," *Autres écrits*, p. 211.

pacity for symbolization, whose space is essentially linguistic, cannot be tackled by the same methods that are used to study the body's functioning.

From this follow a series of epistemological consequences; in particular, any science of man that doesn't take into account the break with nature that was the consequence of the discovery of language is bound to build its conceptual edifice on a faulty premise. Any investigation that doesn't take into account the definition of man as the *talking being* is doomed to failure. We have to get rid of all the systems of belief that are grounded on the illusion of a continuity between biological life, nature, and man.

When humans began to speak 150,000 years ago (according to anthropologists' estimates), this momentous event provoked a tremendous change: it separated humankind from Nature and immersed us in culture: "Not only is language an environment as real as the so-called external world, but [. . .] man grows immersed in a sea of language as well as in the natural world."[21]

From that point on, everything that man encounters, all the objects surrounding him, first go through the symbolic filter of language, even before being concretely experienced. The material world is replaced by a world of words, or, to be more precise, of signifiers: "The world of words creates the world of things."[22]

This separation from nature was complete, including a casting away of what we call animal instinct. Freud was well aware of that fact, since he never used the word in his work (unless under the pen of misguided translators), choosing to use the word *Trieb* in German (in English, *drive*) instead of *instinct*. The drive propels human sexuality in the realm of culture, and subtracts it from the natural world. The animal sexual instinct has only one goal: to insure procreation and hence the preservation of the species. We need only to look around and in ourselves to immediately grasp that human sexuality is far removed from this natural aim, and that even this aim is submitted to diverse symbolic constraints, as Lacan states:

> The effect of language is the cause introduced in the subject. Through this effect, he is not cause of himself, he carries in himself the worm of

---

21. *Autres écrits*, p. 223.
22. *Écrits*, p. 276.

the cause that splits him. The cause of the subject is the signifier without which there wouldn't be any subject in the real [the unconscious]. But this subject is what the signifier represents, and the signifier cannot represent anything but for another subject, to which the subject who listens is reduced.[23]

In other words, to enter the symbolic dimension of language means as well, for man, to be submitted to the effects of the unconscious.

The deleterious consequences of the confusion between material and symbolic processes are numerous; take for example the transference of a Darwinian model of evolution to human societies, a model to which Freud (in *Totem and Taboo*) succumbed against his own theory; or the belief in a biological foundation for language, apparent in the work of Noam Chomsky; or the nostalgia for a return to Mother Nature (what Lacan called the pastoral dimension ever present in culture). These have to be eliminated outright from the social sciences, and the debate recentered on culture, that is to say, in the last analysis, on the symbolic objects made out of language and representations. In the field of psychological inquiry, this illusion of continuity takes the form of a preverbal or ineffable unconscious, that is, a mystery that would have existed before language. Even if there is indeed an unconscious kernel that resists a linguistic formulation, it comes into being after, not before, language; no mysticism, that is, the expression of a preexisting silence, can be grounded on such a notion: "The unconscious is neither primordial nor instinctual; what it knows about the elementary is no more than the elements of the signifier."[24]

As Freud sometimes (but not always) showed, and as Lacan fully demonstrated, any inquiry into human sexuality has to concentrate on its symbolic aspects. Conversely, it is only fitting and coherent that psychoanalysis's contributions to physiology, neurology, and biology should be nil.[25] Psychoanalysis doesn't have the arrogance of going beyond the precise limits of its object.

It is within the restricted framework that psychoanalysis carves for itself that the claim of its scientificity should be addressed, a claim that

---

23. "Position de l'inconscient," *Écrits*, p. 835.
24. *Écrits*, p. 522.
25. *Écrits*, p. 803 (English, p. 302).

Freud never relinquished. He firmly subscribed to the ideal, born with Galileo, of modern science; however, he thought he could find a model for this goal in the natural sciences of the nineteenth century, especially in the field of thermodynamics, as witnessed his constant references to the concept of libido as "energy," the superego as a dam, and the unconscious as a reservoir. If psychoanalysis does not deal with natural objects but with symbolic ones, the methodology of the sciences will fail to account for them. By sticking to a methodology borrowed from nineteenth-century physics (let us emphasize that he had no other possible model at hand), Freud sometimes fell into the trap of seeing a continuity between nature and man.

The model for a scientific construction of psychoanalysis has to be sought elsewhere. If the objects of psychoanalysis are symbolic, they are linguistic in their essence, and therefore the discipline's scientificity depends on the possibility of making linguistics a science. This is what Saussure, unbeknownst to Freud, achieved at the beginning of the twentieth century, and this is why Lacan chose him as one of his first models. If it is possible to submit common language to some form of mathematization, to reduce some of it to pertinent algorithms, then it is possible to assign to psychoanalysis the goal of becoming (but not *in toto*) a science.

The symbols and signifiers with which man surrounds himself are not emanating from nature, objects, infrastructure, or economic production (emanation here would again be an undue transference from the natural world to the cultural sphere). Each time, these symbolic constructs are created inside the realm of linguistic representations. For example, in antiquity, a slave laborer never produced any concept out of his sweat: his work was already taken up in a net of symbolic representations that designated his place, as well as the master's, in the social structure. Similarly, to take up a more recent example, Marxist theory, no amount of toiling by the proletariat can ever give birth to the concept of proletariat. Toiling, unfortunately, does not give birth to ideas—quite the contrary: you need Marx's conceptual and lexical innovation in order for the proletariat to discover itself as proletariat.

But what is the nature of these mental constructs surrounding humanity? Lacan's stance is radical: the symbolic realm is a *fiction*.

"Truth is not internal to a proposition; this makes clear the fictitious character of language."[26] Lacan furthermore differentiates between
the fictions that produce truth and those having to do with exactitude:
"Exactitude has to be distinguished from truth."[27] The term *exactitude* will
be applied only to the results obtained by the method of science (also a
fiction: a mental construction) or, I may add, to everyday life statements
such as "Today, it is snowing";[28] *truth*, on the other hand, will be used
only in social sciences and in psychoanalysis. To make this distinction
clear, let us borrow an example from "Knowledge and Truth,"[29] and let
us consider a rainbow: a scientist can give an exact description of it; for
the poet, however, the truth of the rainbow will be whatever feelings,
memories, and so on its sight inspires in him. In this case, as in many
others, there is no common ground between the exactitude construed by
the scientific description and the truth of the rainbow, even if both can
be grasped as mental constructs: as an exact fiction and as a truth fiction.

This obviously means that the term *fiction* cannot be opposed to
what we mean by *lie* (after all, even a lie hides a truth; it is always uttered for a specific purpose, which we can see as its truth). On the contrary, fiction is the path to either exactitude or truth. Or, as Lacan
declared: "Truth avers itself in a structure of fiction,"[30] that is, neither
truth nor exactitude can preexist their utterance (their fictional construction through a language or algorithm), nor are they "expressed" by
speech or mathematical formulas. Their very existence depends on the
form that determines them.

How then can truth or exactitude be verified? As we have just
seen, not by their internal logic, but by another statement outside of
themselves; this is exactly what modern logic tells us, according to
Tarski, when he writes: "The proposition *it snows* is true if and only
if it snows."[31] No proposition can verify its truth or exactitude by it-

---

26. *Séminaire XVII, L'envers de la psychanalyse*; Paris: Le Seuil, 1991, p. 68.

27. *Écrits*, p. 286.

28. *Ibid.*

29. See Bruce Fink's translation in *Newsletter of the Freudian Field*, Spring–Fall
1989, vol. 3, no. 1–2.

30. See *Autres écrits*, p. 376.

31. See Alfred Tarski, "The Concept of Truth in Formalized Languages," in
Logic, Semantics, Metamathematics, trans. J.-H. Woodger; Oxford: Clarendon Press,
1956, p. 210.

self; truth and exactitude are external to the propositions that utter them.

As Tarski's example shows, a true or exact proposition needs another proposition (not an experiment or a "fact") to be confirmed: "*No factual proposition can ever be proved from an experiment.* Propositions can only be derived from other propositions, they cannot be derived from facts. One cannot prove statements from experiences—'no more than by thumping the table.' This is one of the basic points of elementary logic, but one which is understood by relatively few people even today."[32]

In order to explain Lacan, I assume that, from beginning to end, he aims at coherence and remains faithful to this goal, with one caveat: since we are dealing neither with a philosophical system nor with a "vision of the world" (a *Weltanschauung*), at some point logical coherence will abut its limit; psychoanalysis knows, as does modern science, that no formalization can be all-encompassing.[33]

Second, I contend that Lacan has something to say which is true or exact. When I first read the words that appear on the first page of *Télévision*:[34] "I always tell the truth," I thought I was reading a madman. But what if they were true, what if they had to be, not just struck out as madness, but instead disproven by a reading of the works or some crucial experiment? What if I had to assume that what Lacan says was not a sophistry, a rhetorical wordplay destined to impress, with the proper *kairos*, a naive reader, in order to achieve some imaginary position of superiority? After all, the problem at hand is not what kind of echo Lacan's thought has, or what impression he makes: more importantly, we have to assess if he was and if he still is true or not.

The method I have followed for this book is to anchor the mapping of Lacan's discourse in the formulas, algorithms, boards, and graphs grounded on mathematics and modern logic that are interspersed in his

---

32. Imre Lakatos, "Methodology of Scientific Research Programmes," p. 99, in *Criticism and the Growth of Knowledge*, Imre Lakatos and A. Musgrave, eds.; Cambridge, UK: Cambridge University Press, 1970.

33. As Jonathan Scott Lee writes: "Only by means of an extraordinary explosion of theoretical activity can the limits of theory be revealed and grasped." (*Jacques Lacan*; Amherst, MA: University of Massachussetts Press, 1990, p. 199.

34. "*Télévision*," *Autres écrits*, p. 509. See also the English translation by Denis Hollier, Annette Michelson, and Rosalind Krauss.

entire work. I base this approach on a simple hypothesis: the recourse to mathematical formalization by Lacan is not due to a rhetorical scientism, nor a decoration added more or less by chance to a doctrine, but is the gist of his thought and, as such, has to be taken seriously. I am aware of the dangers such an approach poses; to a humanist reader who has forgotten the mathematics he was taught in college, my book risks appearing dry and too abstract; to a mathematician, simple-minded and contrived. But the benefits outweigh the drawbacks. Lacan aimed for rigor, precision, and exactitude. Lacan did not deal obliquely with discourses, or discourses on discourses in the second or third degree: he spoke and wrote about real things in and of the world even if his topic, the unconscious, remains in the last analysis enmeshed in an impenetrable darkness. This is how I understand such utterances as "The *Écrits* were not meant to be read,"[35] or "A writing is not meant to be understood. You are not obliged to understand my *Écrits*. If you don't understand them, so much the better, it will give you the opportunity to explain them."[36] Simply reading the works would reinsert them in the realm of objects of culture. The belief in understanding would make the statements part of a world of thought that is already known, placing them in harmony with a common sense that is most often incorrect. "Not understanding" is therefore only a prompt for an explanation that makes the work rebellious with respect to a familiar culture, one where everything "goes without saying." To the contrary, in order to access Lacan, we make our own intellectual contribution to the undertaking, to avoid understanding what we have already understood since the beginning.[37]

In that regard, the mathematical formulas have an explanatory power; moreover, they are an essential tool in avoiding the trap of imagery, the idolatry (including Freud's) that Lacan fought all his life. Despite his love for wordplay, stylistic effects, and striking metaphors, his entire work is meant, since its inception, as a bulwark against the inveigling of images. As he said to Serge Leclaire as early as 1954: "Well, you are a little idolater. I will come down from Mount Sinai and smash the tables."[38]

---

35. *Séminaire XX, Encore!*; Paris: Le Seuil, 1975, p. 29.

36. *Séminaire XX*, p. 35 (my translation).

37. *Écrits*, p. 9.

38. *Séminaire II*, p. 73. See Jean-Joseph Goux, "Lacan Iconoclast," in *Lacan and the Human Sciences*, pp. 109–119.

What exactly is the danger here? It is that of projecting an imagery that masks the psyche's real, functioning structure, when to cover up the structure is akin to a repression. We should not drown the subject and the unconscious under an imaginary idolization; images are not only what give a form to our desire, but also what allow us to repress this very desire: "As soon as desire is enmeshed in signifiers, it is a signified desire. And here we all are, fascinated by desire's signification. And we forget the apparatus of signifiers, despite Freud's ministrations."[39]

Lacan, in this regard, walks a fine line between giving his thought the flesh of images and reducing it to its bareness; this is the contradiction that quarters his discourse and gives it its obscurity. Part of this difficulty is explicitly intentional: "I leave the reader no other exit than entering in my text, and I prefer this entrance to be difficult."[40] Another part is unintentional, at least consciously, and the best we can surmise about this difficulty is that he could not do anything else, that something compelled him to expose his theory the way he did.

As for mathematics, the necessity of dealing with it in theoretical psychoanalysis is justified by Lacan this way: "Mathematical formalization is our aim, our ideal. Why? Because it is the only formalization that is a *matheme*, i.e., which is capable of being transmitted in its integrality. Mathematical formalization is writing, but it works only if I present it with the common language I speak."[41]

In other words, transmission by common language is never integral (hence, for Lacan, the essence of communication is misunderstanding); there is always something left out of it (our desire, our unconscious). If we follow a metaphorical path to Lacan's understanding, we run the risk of disseminating his speech without conveying the slightest idea of his discourse (the doctrinal core).[42] When I start from the formulas, graphs, and schemas, I just obey a Lacanian injunction: to get rid of imagery in order to grasp the psyche's structure. The function of the mathematical or topological model goes far beyond that of an illustration or guide for understanding; it aims at *being the subject's structure itself*: "Topology

---

39. *Séminaire III, Les Psychoses*; Paris: LeSeuil, 1981, p. 270.
40. *Écrits*, p. 393.
41. *Séminaire XX*, p. 108.
42. See "Allocution sur l'enseignement," *Autres écrits*, p. 304.

is not there to 'guide us inside the structure' (it is not an image of the structure). Topology *is* the structure."[43]

Lacan therefore pinned his hopes of being heard on mathematical formulas and formal logic: "Truth formalizes itself in science by the way of formal logic; this is for us the model which we have to extend to the structure of language. This is the kernel from which my discourse proceeds."[44]

By insisting on mathematics, Lacan not only attempts to inscribe psychoanalysis in the domain of modern science, but he also breaks away from a form of transmission prevalent until Galileo. We can describe this pedagogy as the "master of Antiquity"; its model would be Plato voicing his teaching to his followers in the academy: in this paradigm, transmission here supposes the co-presence of a master and a disciple, that is, the immediate risk of a double misunderstanding that leaves too much to transference to be really effective.[45] Of course, Lacan never got rid of the philosophical master of Antiquity, since he had disciples listening to the presentation of the formulas and the Borromean knots at his Seminar for twenty-six years. But then, the Seminar could be interpreted as the common language framework for the presentation of mathematical writings, even as it has been a rich source of misunderstandings, which often took the form of disciples' projections on Lacan as a charismatic shaman or a master of all discourses.

In brief, Lacan's recourse to algorithms was aimed at constituting, and then preserving what is integrally transmissible of his doctrine. It aims also at the undoing of the figure of the master of Antiquity—in this case, Lacan's persona, which he lucidly saw as an obstacle to transmission, because it was the focus of his disciples' projections and identifications. We can even infer in Lacan a drive for death, so that the real legacy lives, unencumbered: "This will be said when I'll be dead, which will be the moment when I finally will be heard."[46] Elsewhere, he even hopes to be read when psychoanalysis will have failed: "It is

---

43. "L'étourdit," *Autres écrits*, p. 483.

44. "Allocution sur l'enseignement," *Autres écrits*, p. 302.

45. That is why Lacan cannot be taken for the absolute master of classical, philosophical Antiquity, as *The Absolute Master*, by Mikkel Borch-Jacobsen (himself a philosopher, which explains the misnomer) implies.

46. *Scilicet* 5, 1975, p. 8. Having never known him personally, I am not a disciple of Lacan. Of course, like anybody else, I can fall prey to my own fantasies about Lacan

when psychoanalysis will have been vanquished by the growing impasses of our civilization (a discontent which Freud foresaw) that the indications of my *Écrits* will be taken up again. But by whom?"[47]

At the moment of his death, he said: "I am obstinate . . . I disappear."[48] The core of his thought takes refuge in what is transmissible without contest and without loss, beyond the death of the individual who mapped it out: what is left then to us after his death are the formulas with their obstinate clarity.

Last but not least, the formulas ground Lacan's developments in abstraction, making them capable of the greatest level of generality possible. The more general the formalization, the easier it is to lodge an individual case in it, without forgetting that a case possesses an irreducible singularity that escapes any formalization.

The algorithms, however, do not stand alone as a transmissible knowledge in the works. Side by side with mathematical formalization, there are also what Jean-Claude Milner calls the *logia*:[49] statements that stand out in the discourse's flow through their clarity and numerous reiterations. An example is "The unconscious is structured like a language." According to Milner, the *logia* are recurring, true, essential, and susceptible of being interpreted by themselves. Particular attention should therefore be devoted to them.

I would oppose transmissibility to teaching, and surmise that Lacan's discourse, if it is transmissible, is *not* teachable (following my personal experience and Lacan's lead: "I can be taught only in relation to what I already know, and everybody has known for a long time that teaching is for me learning").[50] What is teaching? It is a process where the teacher learns what he has to teach, while the student can grasp only what he or she already knows. A gap separates the professor and the student, a gap that is usually filled by the imposition of the professor's ideas on the students, who will then passively repeat them in order to pass their exams. Lacan presents us with a different situation; inasmuch

(one of them being that his rationality should impose what he did as self-evident to everybody).

47. "La psychanalyse, raison d'un échec," *Autres écrits*, p. 348.

48. Elisabeth Roudinesco, *Histoire de la Psychanalyse en France*; Paris: Le Seuil, 1986, vol. II, p. 679.

49. Jean-Claude Milner, *L'oeuvre claire*; Paris: Le Seuil, 1995, p. 26 ff.

50. "Allocution sur l'enseignement," *Autres écrits*, p. 299.

as his work says something truly new that has never been heard before, it cannot be taught in a traditional way. A real transmission of Lacan, then, has to be built from scratch on a new conceptual structure, where both student and teacher participate in the discovery.[51]

This book doesn't aim to be exhaustive. Given the sheer mass of Lacan's work and the commentaries it has given birth to, that would be a foolish endeavor. I want to provide a general map to Lacan's thought, a readable synthesis aiming at maximal clarity—perhaps thus incurring the risk of appearing somewhat flatfooted and simpleminded to hardcore Lacanians. Let's also face it: it is hard to write about Lacan—the commentary will never live up to the expectations set by the original text. That is the commentator's destiny, and the challenge he must accept.

One more caveat is necessary here. This is not a book about applied psychoanalysis by a practicing psychoanalyst, or even by somebody who has been analyzed. It is a book about the contribution of theoretical psychoanalysis to science and ethics, a contribution that will survive, I think, even if applied psychoanalysis (the cure) changes or disappears. If science is on its way to the abolition of the subject and the erasure of man, it is the task of theoretical psychoanalysis "to stress in man what in his being depends only on the symbolic order"[52] of language and desire. My hope is that, beyond the generalities of abstractions, practicing psychoanalysts will find echoes of their cases. As far as nonanalysts are concerned, I want to show the incomparable usefulness and relevance of Lacan's psychoanalytical thought to the major questions of our time.

The myopia of the "*explication de texte,*" the derivativeness of a Lacan apprehended primarily through secondary literature, Lacan's bundling with what are called (French) poststructuralism and postmodernism, and the works' literal mistranslation in French commentaries as well as in English translations have often made Lacan's endeavor seem like a castle of fog. This is now so much the case that "a return to Lacan" appears today to be a salutary and necessary move.

---

51. Also, explaining Lacan's theory will have to be distinguished from a cure. As far as a practical psychoanalysis is concerned, the relationship between the student and the teacher is inverted. The analysand *is* the one who knows, whereas the psychoanalyst is there only to facilitate the patient's access to his own unconscious knowledge and to undermine the analysand's transferences. After all, Freud discovered the unconscious only because he listened to his hysterical patients.

52. *Autres écrits*, p. 151.

1

The Structure of the Subject

THE SCHEMA L

By insisting on the notion of *subject*, Lacan follows the distinction introduced by Freud between *ego* and, in German, "*Ich*" (the English *I*). The ego in Freud is only a part of the human subject. In his last elaboration at figuring it, Freud proposed, around 1920, a composition of three agencies: the id, the ego, and the superego. They are anthropomorphic categories: the superego is the internalized image of both parents, the ego represents the individual, and the id is akin to a desiring child. Freud dwelt extensively on the dynamic relations between the agencies that compose a human being, but in the last analysis failed to give us a truly rational description of their interaction. Remaining true to his anthropomorphism, he saw their relationships as akin to interpersonal transactions, with the parents trying to guide the child in the maze of social laws, and the ego acting as a buffer as well as a protector of the inner child. Freud summed up this interaction with a graphic representation that ultimately fails to enlighten us, because it is but a metaphor, caught in the trap of an imaginary representation; if the concepts derive their meaning from their dynamic relations, Freud's imaging (see Fig. 1–1) will only serve to veil the hidden structure of these relations:[1]

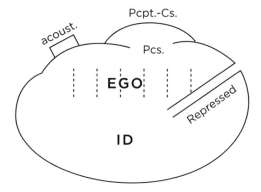

Figure 1–1. Freud's representation of the psyche.

Whereas Freud's scheme is tripartite (id, ego, superego), Lacan's is quaternary; this elaboration with four terms will, at least from the emergence of the *schema L*, be maintained by Lacan throughout the last developments of his theory. Why add a forth term to Freud's three? Following hints in Freud, as well as reflecting on the mirror-stage in the infant, Lacan posits that the ego receives its first consistence through a reflected image: this is something that is other, so much more so that the "other" image is the support for the mother's gaze. Hence, the Imaginary order always implies *two* objects, an ego (*o* object) and an other (*o'* object), hence the fourth term added to build a quaternary structure.

---

1. Freud, *The Ego and the Id*; New York: Norton, 1960, p. 18. "Let us say it is not the best thing that Freud did" ("Le Séminaire de Caracas," in *L'Âne* 1, p. 30); see also the critique of "dam" and "energy" in "Télévision," *Autres écrits*, p. 522: "The Freudian primary process is not something that is numbered, but something that is deciphered: jouissance itself. Jouissance then cannot be transformed in energy, and cannot be written as such." For a detailed exposition of Lacan's theory of the subject, see Bruce Fink's well-informed *The Lacanian Subject*; Princeton University Press, 1995.

But how do the new orders correlate? Lacan proposed two main ways to describe their relationships. The first one is the schema L', whose complete development is first found in the "Seminar on the Purloined Letter" (1956)[2] (see Fig. 1–2):

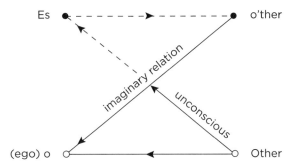

Figure 1–2. Lacan, Schema L. The (Es) S is in reference to Freud's unconscious. ("Wo Es war, soll Ich Werden.")

If we compare this schema to Freud's, a series of qualitative differences jump out at us, the first of which is that Lacan's agencies are not submitted to a graphical analogy, but are tied together through directional vectors (a way of representing the force of the drives) that at the same time identify their respective functions and relationship. When Freud thought about the drives of the unconscious, he considered them either as mythological beings (Eros and Thanatos) or through the notion of forces derived from nineteenth-century thermodynamics. As Freud's diagram, which I would call a "psychic potato," is a projection, his descriptions of the psychic apparatus are often metaphors.

With Lacan, we are dealing with vector analysis.[3] At first glance, the vectors define two axes: the axis of the symbolic/unconscious order, and the axis of the imaginary relationship. The first one, the unconscious,

2. *Écrits*, p. 53.

3. For those who are interested in the history of ideas, the possibilities of vectorial analysis are already portended in 1947 ("La psychiatrie anglaise et la guerre," *Autres écrits*, p. 107).

is marked by its radical Otherness, its exteriority (language as a structure is not "inside" an individual), and its materiality (signifiers are always concrete).[4] We can also define this unconscious axis as the vector of the Law (of language), which imposes itself on desire and therefore creates it, beyond the grasp of any individual, conscious decision.

This vector makes the dialectical relation between law and desire crystal clear. No desire can exist without repression, and no repression can subsist without desire, to the point that desire will create obstacles to its realization just to survive. Of this dialectical nature of desire and law, Lacan says: "The Name of the Father is the vector of an incarnation of the Law in desire."[5]

Lacan illustrates this dialectics by a brilliant paraphrase of Saint Paul, where the Thing of psychoanalysis, that is, the mother, replaces the Pauline concept of sin:[6] "Is the Law identical to the Thing? Absolutely not. However, I have known the Thing only through the Law. Indeed, I would not have fancied to lust for the Thing if the Law hadn't said—Thou shalt not lust. [. . .] Without the Law the Thing is dead."[7]

Let us now place these exigencies in the schema L' (see Fig. 1–3):

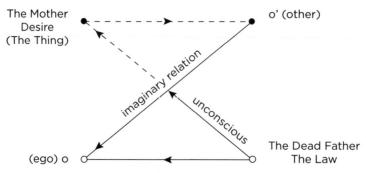

Figure 1–3. Schema L with exigencies.

From this follows the notion of the unconscious as entirely cultural; no speaking being will lack an unconscious, no animal will be

4. See the developments in Chapter 2 of this volume.

5. "Note sur l'enfant," *Autres écrits*, p. 373.

6. A substitution that made Lacan particularly proud: "I have replaced sin by the Thing," he once said.

7. *Séminaire VIII, L'éthnique de la psychanalyse*; Paris: Le Seuil, 1986, p. 101.

gifted with one. The vector formalizes the Freudian distinction between animal instinct and human desire and drives; desire is a concept devoid of any naturalness.

The schema makes clear the problem of double inscription of any signifier in the psychic apparatus: it will always represent at the same time a desire and its interdiction; it is a compromise. Freud called this double inscription overdetermination; to flesh it out, we will borrow an example from *The Interpretation of Dreams*:

> The hysterical vomiting of a female patient proved, on the one hand, to be the fulfillment of an unconscious fantasy from the years of puberty—namely, the wish that she might be continually pregnant, and have a multitude of children; and this was subsequently supplemented by the wish that she might have them by as many fathers as possible. Against this immoderate wish arose a powerful defensive reaction. But just as by vomiting the patient might have spoilt her figure and her beauty, so that she would no longer find favor in any man's eye, the symptom was also in keeping with the punitive trend of thought, and so, being admissible on both sides it was allowed to become a reality.[8]

The vector defines the subject of the unconscious, for the time being noted S by homophony with Freud's *Es, Id* in German. Later, to indicate its nature divided between consciousness and unconscious, Lacan will write it with a bar: *S*. The unconscious vector gives a representation for Freud's *Id thinks*, that is, the discovery that upset all conceptions of thought as equivalent to consciousness that had been accepted up to the publication of *Interpretation of Dreams*.

The second axis defines the imaginary relationship; this is where the old notion of consciousness is displaced and completely reformulated.

The repressed subject finds its incarnation in objects, *o'* and *o*, by which the ego defines itself in a specular image,[9] and by which it creates its autonomy, unity, and totality at an early age. Since these qualities all depend on a premature image that anticipates real motor skills, the constitution of the ego has all the characteristics of a narcissistic

---

8. Freud, *The Interpretation of Dreams*, translated and edited by A. A. Brill, *The Basic Writings of Sigmund Freud*; New York: The Modern Library, 1995, p. 512.

9. See "The Mirror Stage," *Écrits, a Selection*, trans. Alan Sheridan; New York: Norton, 1977, pp. 1–7.

fiction that will mark all stages of further development. At the beginning, it is the mother's gaze on the infant that gives to the *o* object its first incarnation; it is then superseded by other objects, whose range in human desire is infinite.

In their turn, these objects will define the ego, by way of the imaginary relationship, that is, as the sum total of projections and identifications. Our ego is what we dream it to be (how we have internalized the way we incarnate our drives). If the ego defines consciousness, then consciousness, and the reality it supports, is a dream (a projection or an identification); as Lacan says, "Reality is what we lean on in order to go on dreaming."[10] Here its repressive function can be pointed out: the images (objects) that the ego surrounds itself with not only inadequately represent desire, they are made in order to forget desire. That is why the vector supporting the imaginary relationship cuts through the vector of the unconscious that originates from the Symbolic order.

The imaginary axis is where fantasies are aligned. If we can locate the dead father in the Symbolic order, and the mother in the Real, then the child will occupy the axis of the Imaginary order. Indeed, the child is the *o* object of the mother's desire, as well as the subject of his or her own desire, as prohibited by the Law. Such a structurally conflicted position (desired as well as desiring) can't help but produce symptoms: one can go so far as to affirm that a child is a symptom of the parental agencies. The symptom will testify to the truth of the parents' desire as well as to the child's: the symptom "represents" the truth.[11]

In the schema L (see p. 4), the difference between what we can perceive and what we can't is marked by the opposition between the full and dotted line. The points are either full or empty; fullness indicates an existence that is beyond our grasp because it is unconscious; emptiness defines the impossibility that our objects encounter when they try to signify our desire. The first vector (unconscious), starting from language (the Symbolic), makes crystal clear that the Symbolic order is the space where everything begins. Also, since it creates and defines the *Es*, it draws upon the realm of the unconscious. Hence, marked

---

10. "Discours à l'E.P.F.," *Scilicet* 2–3, 1970, p. 28.

11. *Autres écrits*, p. 373: "The symptom may represent the truth of the family couple."

by a fundamental otherness, the vector clarifies Lacan's statement that man's desire is the desire for the Other, as well as the desire of the Other.

The ego receives its signification(s) from the projections and identifications (the imaginary relationship) it builds with its other, the o' object. Since its *meaning* is unconscious, it is an empty set: only an imaginary *signification* is accessible to the ego. .

It is now time to give an approximation of what the o object is. At first, Lacan gives it the privilege of constituting psychoanalysis as a scientific discipline; then the o object, accompanied by various formalizations, is the foundation for the hope that psychoanalysis will approximate a science.[12] This difference between psychoanalysis and scientific inquiry is made obvious by the very nature of the o object: it is not to be confused with an object in the world (the object of a science, the object of a philosophy, or more generally anything falling under our senses' perception) since it is affected by the unconscious; in other words, a psychoanalytical object will always have two sides: one that is observable, and one that escapes the grasp of consciousness.

In the schema L, o appears as the ego, constituted by the two vectors of the Symbolic and Imaginary orders. It thus possesses a dual aspect, conscious and unconscious, and its inscription in the psyche is double, or, as Freud would say, it is overdetermined. Moreover, it receives its quality from the mirror image, o'.

In the history of the subject, the o object is the first moment (hence the *a* that manifests its primacy in French) that is identified by the child as a signifier of or for his mother's desire and love; the mother's breast, glance, or voice, where the child tries to find a proof of her love, the feces being offered as a reciprocating gift to her. The object here is the mark of a loss; representing a mother with whom complete fusion is impossible, it offers a substitute satisfaction that is quartered between frustration and jouissance. This alienation of the mother's objects is strengthened because all of them have at one point or another to be forfeited through weaning, distance, and finally separation.

Inasmuch as all objects of desire will later be substituted for these primary metonymies (voice, gaze, breast), the o object is the cause of desire. Given the infinite number of objects (people—but as signifiers—images, etc.) human desire aspires to, o may be almost anything.

---

12. *Séminaire XI*, p. 23.

The *o object* finds its definition at the level of the Imaginary order, and in that sense an object is only a representation (a projection or an identification). Hence, the objects we desire in the world are unconsciously constructed by ourselves: they participate in the structure of the subject. Their otherness is relative to our imaginary projections and identifications, and they are essentially narcissistic. Against this unconscious process, the ego is the strongest defense: "The dialectics of misknowledge, of denial and of narcissistic alienation are due to the ego."[13]

Inasmuch as the *o* object only partially represents our desire, it is a metonymy. But this metonymy is not a part for a whole, which would be the mother, the body, or the unconscious: the *o* object is a metonymy (that is, a synechdoche) because it represents only in part the function (desire) that produces it.[14] The object is fundamentally (and unavoidably) an alienation of desire—it just masks the inability of any object to fulfill desire: "The object of psychoanalysis is not man; it is what he lacks—not an absolute lack, but the lack of an object."[15] Later, Lacan will condense this loss in a striking formula: "The object is failure."[16]

The *o* object as conceived by Lacan renders any "objectivation" or objectivity in psychoanalysis impossible. The *o* object is always entangled in the structure, and submitted to the determinations of the partially unconscious signifying chain, on which we have very little influence. It cannot be detached from these determinations for objective consideration. It is always a symptom of the observer or the observed, and no metalanguage is at hand to allow for its objective consideration; the pretense to objectivity is very often a means of repression of the singular unconscious desire that motivates our choice of a particular object. This does not mean that truth is unattainable, of course; it is just hidden and designated at the same time by the object as symptom: "In psychoanalysis, no objectivation is possible, because the subject is always implied in his objects."[17]

---

13. *Écrits*, p. 454.
14. *Écrits*, p. 817.
15. "Réponses à des étudiants en philosophie," *Autres écrits*, p. 211.
16. *Séminaire XX*, p. 55.
17. *Écrits*, p. 861.

This implication takes an apparently paradoxical form: "The subject is in internal exclusion to his object."[18] If we go back to the schema L, the *o* object appears at the end of a drive vector originating in the exteriority and otherness of the unconscious vector, as well as the point of origin of the interiority we call ego. This double inscription of the *o* object can be called the "extimacy" of the object: it is the opposite of intimacy.

We can also illustrate the schema L in a historical (albeit hypothetical) way. The first word uttered must have been a "No!" How can I be so sure of an event for which we will forever lack forensic evidence? It is pretty simple: we learn from anthropology, ethnography, and history that there is only one prohibition that spans all human cultures and civilizations: the prohibition of incest. The most primitive as well as the most advanced cultures on the face of the earth all share the dread of incest.

Hence it must have been the edict about incest that was the first word uttered. This "no" gives birth to humanity, and separates us from animal instinct. Deprived of language, animals cannot formulate such a symbolic interdiction. From the originary moment, instinct in human beings will be transformed into drive. This led Freud to introduce the term *drive* (in German, *Trieb*) in the "Three Contributions to the Theory of Sexuality," published in 1905. From that point on, *Instinkt* will be reserved exclusively for the animal, *Trieb* for human beings; Lacan follows course. The birth of humanity cannot be separated from the birth of language as interdiction. This allows Lacan to give a tremendous extension to the Freudian concept of castration: it appears as soon as we (men and women) speak, that is, as soon as we are inserted in the symbolic order that makes the prohibition of incest possible.[19]

Freud and Lacan differ in the originary scenarios they propose; for Freud, the first instant of humanity was the murder of the Father: "In the beginning was the deed" is the last sentence of *Totem and Taboo* (1960): here, the deed is the acting out of the desire to eliminate the father as incarnating the prohibition against the sons, who don't have access to the primal herd's females. Even if Lacan dismisses the quest

---

18. *Ibid.*
19. See *Écrits*, p. 852.

for a beginning of humanity as futile, we can infer from his construction what an originary Lacanian moment would have been; it cannot be a deed, because a deed cannot produce a concept, only a concept can. So, for Lacan, in the beginning was the word, and this word is the one that kills the father as a thing and promotes him to his symbolic dimension: "The symbol manifests itself as the murder of the thing, and this death constitutes the subject as eternally desiring."[20] Nothing makes the cultural nature of desire (as opposed to the naturalness of instinct) clearer. Whereas an animal's sexuality aims at one unique goal, reproduction and continuation of the species, human sexuality, because of its inherent cultural nature, is not bound to reproduction, but answers to the linguistically articulated Law of repression: hence the immense variety of objects that the drives may choose to substitute for the first, prohibited, and lost object that is the mother.

This leads Lacan to a redefinition of paternity in which, first and foremost, to be a father has to do with naming. Whereas there is an empirical certainty about who is the mother of a child, the Romans would say *pater semper incertum*—the father is always uncertain. Hence, paternity (before DNA testing) has to be grounded by naming who the child's father is. This is why the Bible, for example, gives a lot of attention to patrilinearity: this attention is the symptom of an uncertainty, and hence the symbolic and linguistic nature of paternity: it is in itself an abstraction, a place, a function that a specific father (but also a woman) can fill—or not.

Why not, then, a living father? Could it be that the simple act of naming (of inscribing something in the Symbolic agency) has to do with killing? Hegel said as much, and Freud thought so too, as he wrote in *Totem and Taboo*. However, the father of the primal herd of advanced primates was never killed by the sons who wanted to share the female apes. Somebody was promoted to the Name of the Father, in effect killing him as an individual and making of him an abstract principle: the Law that prohibits incest.

Which leads us to the opposing pole of the vector: the mother. She is constituted as the first object of the (male or female) child's desire by the prohibition itself. It is because of the Law that she exists. The

---

20. *Écrits*, p. 319.

mother is not a natural object: the prohibition of incest constitutes her also as a cultural one. A cursory glance at animal societies will confirm that the human concepts of "father" and "mother" have no relevance at all.

At the same time, since she is effectively interdicted by the Law, she is also the first *lost* object of desire. In that sense, she will be substituted for in the course of life by a series of other objects meant to evoke her (*o* in the schema), objects that are bound always to be poor representations of the Supreme Good she once incarnated for the child.

Since the mother is always lost through and by the very objects that are supposed to represent her, she cannot be given the status of an object herself. Lacan, in *L'éthique de la psychanalyse* (*Séminaire VIII*), gives her a status beyond language, the status of an unconscious thing.

The dialectics of the Symbolic and Imaginary orders lead us to distinguish need, request (demand),[21] and desire.

Need will be reserved for what insures our self preservation and reproduction. Nevertheless, in the human sphere, needs cannot be confused with animal instincts: they are submitted to the signifier, as is everything in our world: "Desire is not articulable in speech; but it is articulated in language."[22] In particular, need is submitted to request, which is what we can articulate with regard to our desire. Indeed, it can be said that desire, as structured by language, is what replaces need in humankind:

"Desire results from the necessity, for the subject, to submit his needs to the procession of the signifier."[23] Hence, "Desire and request radically reshape need."[24] Request, in this framework, is always a metonymy, an articulation of desire that can have no pretense to represent it all. That is why Lacan warns the psychoanalyst about answering the analysand's request; the request, in fact, cannot be satisfied by any answer or object: "If the psychoanalyst cannot answer the request, it is because what is requested is an Other Thing."[25]

---

21. All the translations up to this date translate the French *demande* by "demand." But "demand" translates the French *exigence*, and thus *demande* should be rendered in English by "request."

22. *Autres écrits*, p. 171.

23. *Écrits*, p. 628.

24. *Autres écrits*, p. 224.

25. *Autres écrits*, p. 343.

THE SCHEMA R

Five years after the schema L, Lacan proposes another representation for the structure of the subject, the *schema R* (see Fig. 1–4):[26]

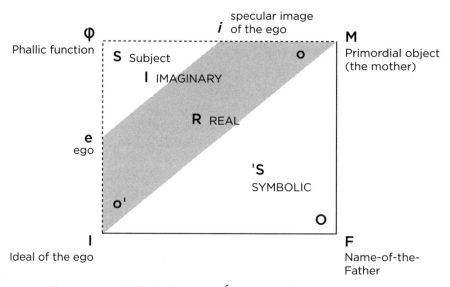

Figure 1–4. The Schema R, *Écrits*, p. 553 (my translation).

This schema can be easily superposed with the schema L; the four
corners O, S, o', and o are the four points of the schema L; they are
specified by four functions: the Name-of-the-Father describes the
Other, the phallic function (that is, castration) the unconscious subject, the Mother the o object, the Ideal of the ego the o' object; the ego
and its specular image allow for the construction of a Möbius strip (see
p. 20 of this volume).

The schema R also organizes and distinguishes the orders which,
from that point on, will be the Lacanian doctrine's theoretical anchoring points, and those by which he distinguishes his contribution from
Freud's: "My three orders are not Freud's; they are the Real, the Symbolic and the Imaginary";[27] these respectively replace the id, the super-

---

26. *Écrits*, p. 553 (1955–1956).
27. *Ibid.*

ego, and the ego. Hence Lacan's is neither a simple act of renaming, nor a replacement of Freud's concepts by synonyms. He produces homonyms (here, new names without equivalent in the Freudian topography) by completely redrawing the relations between the agencies, even if their content is roughly analogous.

Before we get to their interactions, however, we need to define each of the three Lacanian orders (or sets, in mathematical terms) according to a property they don't share with the two others; this is the only way to make them absolutely distinct.[28] Let the reader beware that a formal definition is here but a first step; the sets will receive their precise meaning only when they are put in relationship to one another, when the static description is superseded by a dynamics.

R (the Real) = there is . . .
S (the Symbolic agency) = there is difference
I (the Imaginary agency) = there is similarity

The Symbolic Order

We can equate the *Symbolic order* with the set of signifiers according to a strict Saussurean view: language is but the sum of negative differences, and signification and meaning are produced by the comparison of those differences without content. But Lacan, compared to Saussure, gives a tremendous extension to the concept of signifier, since any object in the human sphere is marked by the pregnancy of language and thus must be conceived as a signifier. Also, he stresses the supremacy of the Symbolic order: for him, it is the foundation of all psychic mechanisms. Developing the distinction, made by Saussure, between language and speech, and thus underlining language's transindividual nature, Lacan posits the Symbolic order's radical otherness by designating it as the Other; at first external to subject, then interiorized, the Symbolic order determines the subject by its signifying chains, undermining the ego's autonomy. Indeed, the ego is submitted to a radical determinacy that it chooses to largely ignore.

---

28. See Jean-Claude Milner's lucid exposé in *Les noms indistincts*; Paris: Le Seuil, 1983, p. 7. See also Jean-Pierre Cléro's very clear book, *Le vocabulaire de Lacan*; Paris: Ellipses, 2002.

The Symbolic order is a universal characteristic of humanity; a group can be said to be human only if it is subordinated to a symbolic structure. At the same time, this mark of humanity is specified according to linguistic groups: any existing language determines a symbolic order particular to a certain community. At the level of the Symbolic order resides the broadest level of generality: this is where general statements can be made, where, through a given language, societies put their signifiers in common; this is where the superego and cultural constraints function. This is also where we can place history, inasmuch as symbolic orders vary from culture to culture and era to era. For example, the function of the father is not the same before and after DNA testing; scientific determination of paternity influences its symbolic dimension.

The Imaginary Order

The *Imaginary order* is the set of similarities, that is, in psychoanalytic terms, the set of projections and identifications. It builds a world of representations and objects by actualizing the possibility of representing from the Symbolic order; hence Lacan denies it any autonomy and any possibility of totalization. The function of the Imaginary order is to represent what we call reality, which we must then distinguish from the Real (see below), inasmuch as it has a strongly fictitious essence.

The Symbolic order's theoretical position of supremacy, especially over the Imaginary order, is justified by the fact, in a world where "words create things." Submitting the ego (and, with it, the Imaginary order) to an absolute psychic determinism originating in the Symbolic order and working in the real logically leads Lacan to a undermining of the notions of hope and happiness; in "*Télévision*," to Jacques-Alain Miller's question ("What can I hope?"),[29] he answers first that hope must specify an object; he then denies any hope in a political revolution; he shows, moreover, that happiness depends on good luck (in French, *bonheur* = *bon heur*, the "good time" that can happen—or not); this imprevisibility is enough to negate hope. As far as theoretical psychoanalysis is concerned, Lacan's hope is reduced to a good transmission through mathematics; the goal of an analytical cure is only to put the analysand in a position where he can with-

---

29. "Télévision," *Autres écrits*, pp. 542–543.

stand and accept his sexual unhappiness, provided he desires to tolerate his unconscious contradictions.

These goals are indeed modest and specific; however, one cannot help inscribing these restrictions in a vaster constellation, where the belittling of the ego and the Imaginary is in fact the figure for a repression of the notions of freedom, freedom of choice, happiness, hope, belief in a better future—in brief, the foundations of the *American way of life*, often criticized by Lacan. It would be easy to show that Lacan apprehends America only through his critique of the ego psychology imported by the analysts fleeing Nazism before World War II. His America is a moralizing fiction, an imaginary construct, which in the end produces a blindness to the successes of American happiness. Insistence on pure theory, on the Symbolic order and the Real at the expense of Imaginary (but successful) fictions satisfies here a certain Old World haughtiness, justified by the theory but leading to impotence on a pragmatic level. Here, Lacan's denunciation of capitalistic alienation by and in merchandise-objects falls flat,[30] since in his construct any object represents a frustration of desire; one can differentiate between "bad" and "worse" alienation through objects only by reference to a moral system that Lacan repudiates anyway.

Such a view makes change an almost unthinkable notion, except at the level of a psychoanalytic restructuring of the individual. Changes in the Symbolic order, such as the creation of modern science or Freud's discovery of the unconscious, are few and far between; changes in the Imaginary order are always illusory, in that they leave the structure intact: there is no retroactive return of the Imaginary order to the Symbolic. For example, a political revolution, for Lacan, leaves intact the function of the sovereign in the social structure, even if the master changes place with the oppressed. It may well be that Lacan indicated by this conservatism the precise limits of the theory and practice of pyschoanalysis; however, it is a fact that the supremacy of the Symbolic order leaves little place for progress and little hope for change and freedom of choice. In the end, at the level of social problems, the pragmatic function of the Imaginary order is denied because it is denounced as an illusion, a fantasy, or an error. Lacan, in this case, voids practical solutions of any success according to a moral presupposition that always

---

30. "Radiophonie," *Autres écrits*, p. 435.

gives precedence to theory, and to the structure of a Symbolic order that cannot be modified by the exercise of free will. What has to be grasped here is that the validity of this presupposition (supremacy of the structure) is not weightier than its opposite (emphasis on free will) on the ethical level. Simply said, in certain circles, pessimism is more chic than optimism; but a pragmatic solution to a problem is no less efficacious because it is fictitious and/or illusory, and high theory may be what covers up our impotence.

The attribution of a positive value to the Symbolic order's supremacy, and the emphasis on structure versus imaginary change can be read as a moralization whose historical effect is to build an opposition between France, the land of structure, and the United States, the land of the imaginary. It is a leap of faith to deduce, from the logical antecedence and the logical supremacy of the Symbolic order, its ethical priority.

Lacan indeed belittles all the successes accomplished through imaginary fictions; yet even if our liberty, our possibility of creating wealth, our choices for a better future depend on a fictitious agency, that doesn't make them less successful. Nevertheless, the supremacy of the Symbolic order is sometimes for Lacan the way to exalt an Old World pessimism, where progress is tied down by tradition, against a New World pragmatism, whose undeniable successes justify a boundless faith in the future. In fact, the critique of ego psychology in the name of the supremacy of the Symbolic order (even if theoretically correct) is also used by Lacan to reject America, "a society where values are scaled according to the income tax,"[31] a rejection he shares with countless French intellectuals.

The Real

The *Real* is not an agency or an order; it is a set whose contents are unknown. That is why it cannot be defined otherwise than by an affirmation of existence ("There is . . .") that cannot be qualified in any way; what there is, we don't know, because it remains hidden from us in the unconscious. There are meaning and truth in the unconscious (as opposed to significations, which for Lacan proceed from the Imagi-

---

31. "Réponse à des étudiants de philosophie," *Autres écrits*, p. 206.

nary order, and hence are essentially fictitious), but they are out of the reach of our consciousness. The Real is therefore what escapes any formalization and any representation (this definition of the Real by pyschoanalysis is quite close to the one used for reality in science, that is, what escapes formalization). It is only through lapsi, evocations, silences, dreams, that we may have an inkling of the Real. We know it exists, but we don't know the content of this existence: "It is enough for us to posit that the unconscious *is*, no more and no less."[32] Like the Symbolic agency, on which the Real's existence depends, the Real is external to the subject, and, as such, it is also truly Other, a radical difference that we cannot reduce to our usual (imaginary) ways of understanding.

As opposed to the generalities grounded in the Symbolic order, it is in the Real where we find singularities. The psychoanalytic Real is shared by none, it is unique to each individual (no one can dream the same dream someone else does). Here, Lacan has to be strongly opposed to Jung, who, through his idea of unconscious archetypes, in fact inverted the Freudian doctrine; the unconscious in Jung is a community of symbols, whereas Freud, and more clearly Lacan, makes the unconscious the locus of a singular desire without form and words; for Freud and Lacan, there is no collective unconscious; archetypes belong first to the Symbolic order. Jung makes of the unconscious a reservoir of myths, thereby completely erasing the core of Freud's discovery; Jungian psychoanalysis is but an avatar of mythological (or primitive) thinking, a model that cannot be inscribed in the realm of modern science and one that gives birth to a series of deleterious confusions.

We cannot baptize the Real as an *order* or an *agency*, precisely because we don't know its contents; we know only their consequences and repercussions. This is where sense can also be reversed in *nonsense*, where signifiers are pulverized and atomized, as opposed to the Imaginary order, where signifieds give us the impression of consistency, as leading to the distinction, in Lacan, between the unconscious Real and the "reality" of the Imaginary order.

Lacan worked through several definitions of the unconscious during his life. They are not to be considered as contradictory, but as variants on a coherent and persistent theme. The unconscious is not a being: "We don't even know if the unconscious has a proper being, and

---

32. "Radiophonie," *Autres écrits*, p. 432.

it is because we could not say 'what it is' that we have given it the name of Id (*Es* in German)."[33] In other words, the unconscious is a pure locus without the derived properties attributable to a being, it is not a philosophical substance to which we could attribute qualities or properties. It has to be dissociated from the notion of being at the center of philosophy (in particular in its latest incarnation in Heidegger).

Therefore, it cannot be reduced to what is *not* consciousness,[34] even by the negation implied by the word "unconscious"; that is why, in *Télévision*, Lacan points out the unsatisfactory negative nature of the word we have inherited from Freud, while acknowledging that we will have to make do with it.[35]

Since the very existence of the unconscious depends on the Symbolic order, which is external to us, the unconscious is not interiority, nor an "inner world," an underground, or an inside full of mysteries we carry and that could be anatomically localizable. This can be derived directly from the often-repeated sentence, "The unconscious is structured like a language," or its variant "The unconscious is the discourse of the Other, structured like a language."[36] To posit the symbolic structure of language is equivalent to positioning the unconscious as Other (radically external). Language being external to man,[37] the bits of linguistic matter we can detect in the unconscious are also outside "us." To put this in another way, if there is no unconscious before the emergence of language,[38] and language is external to the brain, then the unconscious is also external: "The exteriority of the Symbolic order in regard to the person is the notion of the unconscious itself."[39]

The unconscious is therefore not a hidden, internal soul. Since Aristotle's *De anima*, the concept of soul has served as a metonymy of

---

33. "La méprise du sujet supposé savoir," *Autres écrits*, p. 333.

34. *Écrits*, p. 830.

35. "Télévision," *Autres écrits*, p. 511.

36. See, among numerous examples, "Petit discours à l'ORTF," *Autres écrits*, p. 223. Lacan notes that the expression "structured like a language" is pleonastic, since a language is a material structure.

37. "The linguistic material is everywhere else than in the brain." ("Discours de Rome," *Autres écrits*, p. 148). Its location is in libraries, bookstores, computers, on TV, in our speech, and so on.

38. "The unconscious is neither primeval nor instinctual." *Écrits*, p. 522.

39. *Écrits*, p. 469.

the person, the internal locus where thinking takes place. Since thinking is only composed by and of signifiers, and nothing else, and since the Symbolic order of the signifiers is external, the interiority of man's soul is a concept belonging (as is well attested) to the philosophy of Antiquity, operating by unconfirmed hypothesis as the "sum total of its functions for the body."[40]

What remains beyond discourse—the unconscious—no longer constitutes an interiority, since it is simply a hole dug and then veiled by language. The other side of truth is not something unutterable or ineffable or preverbal: "Truth can be told only in half, because, beyond this half said, there is nothing to say. [. . .] Here, in consequence, discourse disappears. We don't speak about what is unutterable."[41]

If there is a linguistic structure in the unconscious, then there is knowledge in it: "The unconscious is to not remember what one knows."[42] This is where the negative Freudian notion of the *Unbewusstsein* can be partially justified, but only by considering the functioning of the unconscious, which, through repression, in fact negates itself: "The Real induces its own failure of recognition, indeed produces its systematic negation."[43]

Finally, the logion "The Real is impossible (*L'impossible, c'est le réel*)"[44] refers to the ultimate impenetrability of the unconscious. It is what resists any further inquiry, what escapes any formulation, exactly as, in the end, matter escapes the ultimate grasp of modern physics. This has nothing to do with an ineffable mystical experience, or a pleasant sally, but everything to do with the definition of impossibility given by modern logic: "The real in an experience of speech appears only through a virtuality, which in the edifice of logic is defined as an impossibility."[45]

---

40. "Télévision," *Autres écrits*, p. 512.

41. *Séminaire XVII*, p. 58. This will have consequences in the approach toward feminine sexuality; what is not said in feminine jouissance is not some unspeakable Eternal Feminine, but just a relationship to a logical or mathematical void, which differs from nothingness. See "*Proposition sur le psychanalyste de l'École*," *Autres écrits*, p. 250.

42. "La méprise du sujet supposé savoir," *Autres écrits*, p. 333.

43. "Proposition sur le psychanalyste de l'École," *Autres écrits*, p. 244.

44. *Séminaire XVII*, p. 192.

45. "Allocution sur les psychoses de l'enfant," *Autres écrits*, p. 366. The impossibility and the void will be described later by Lacan as the absence of sexual rapport.

Potentially, the schema R allows for another representation of the subject of the unconscious; if we cut the strip of the Real, effectuate a half-turn torsion, and glue the extremities, we have built a Möbius strip (see Fig. 1–5):

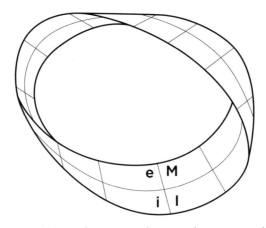

Figure 1–5. The Möbius strip that can be extracted from the Schema R (see p. 12 of this volume)

What was a bidimensional description is now an object in four dimensions,[46] but with one surface and one line of demarcation. This line repeats both the figures of the triangles of the unconscious subject *Phi*, *i*, *e*, and of the Other and other O, *o*, *o'*. On the strip's surface, we can inscribe an *o* object and then immediately understand its double inscription (what Freud called overdetermination), conscious and unconscious, as signified and signifier, or its inscription on the Imaginary and the Symbolic side.

---

46. See Nathalie Charraud, "Mathématiques lacaniennes," in *Qui sont vos psychanalystes?*, J.-A. Miller, ed.; Paris: Le Seuil, 2002, p. 390.

A psychoanalytic interpretation will be a slice cut from the strip, one that will show that any signifier has a reverse (an unconscious meaning). The interpretative cut in fact shows that it has an inscription both on the side of the Symbolic-unconscious axis and on that of the Imaginary axis, remodeling in a rigorous way the Freudian double inscription.

This leads Lacan to assert that only psychoanalysis can, by interpretation, show that any discourse has a reverse,[47] another side.

THE GRAPHS OF DESIRE

To further clarify the elaboration made possible by the schema L', Lacan will later propose a variation in the form of the graphs of desire, in "Subversion of the Subject and Dialectics of Desire in the Freudian Unconscious" (read first at a colloquium in 1960) (see Figs. 1–6 and 1–7):

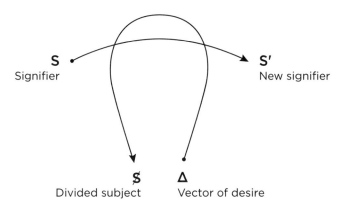

Figure 1–6. The first graph of desire (*Écrits*, p. 805, my English additions).

---

47. "Radiophonie," *Autres écrits*, p. 418.

The vector of the signifying chain (S → S') crosses the vector of desire (Δ ↔ $, the split subject). To illustrate this abstract representation with an example, let us see how we could inscribe a person's utterance (e.g., "I love you") in it:

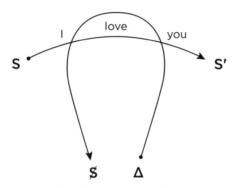

Figure 1–7. The first graph of desire, an example.

This representation is but a flattening of what happens when we speak. When I say "I love you" to somebody, I provoke an anticipation and a retroaction that need time to develop to make the meaning of what I say clear; the anticipation begins with the very first word: the "I" utterance at the same time defines the speaking subject in relationship to the addressee, and creates an expectation about what it is going to do. Then the verb "love" creates another anticipation. Then comes "you," the object that resolves the anticipation. By retroaction, my interlocutor and I can begin to build the meaning of the statement; the sentence is immediately reread backwards in order to make sense. It is only when the sentence is complete that the double processes of anticipation and retroaction can come to the provisional closure of signification.

The figure also makes clear the necessity that requires desire to be submitted to the constraint of the signifying chain, and so to escape the naturalness of animal instinct. What is equally clear are the repressive nature of speech and the constitution of objects with regard to desire: the subject will be barred from access to his/her full realization of his/her desire in exactly the same way as the signifying vector cuts through the vector of desire, thereby producing a divided subject that is no longer able to adhere fully to its desire.

The two anchoring points where the subject and the object intersect with desire also manifest what has been said earlier about double inscription.

Whereas the signifying chain has a diachronic aspect (i.e., it needs time to pass from one metonymy of desire to another, or, more simply, a sentence needs time to be heard) the other axis is synchrony: this is where metaphor, the substitution of one signifier by another, reigns, without regard to time. Indeed, time itself is an imaginary representation, from the point of view of the Freudian or Lacanian unconscious, which does not know time.[48]

In light of Lacan's subsequent elaboration, it is possible for us to understand the limitations of the schema L' as well as of the graphs of desire. One of them is its bidimensionality, which prevents any conception of the void essential to the fields of both truth and exactitude, as we have seen. The void, in the 1954 schema, is present only in the circles marking the ego and the Other, not between the exigencies; therefore, at this point their relationship has to be conceived as full. But more importantly, the schema L' and, afterward, the schema R', veil the subject's real structure by an intuitive, geometrical perception. In other words, being nontopological, they participate in the Imaginary order.[49] Hence the necessity of a transformation or evolution from an intuitive geometry to a topology that can overcome the imaginary aspects of the schemas to ground them in the logic of the Symbolic order.

---

48. I leave aside three further elaborations of the graph, found in *Écrits*.

49. As Miller emphasizes in his commentary on Lacan's diagrams in *Écrits*, p. 903. The following draws on my "Introduction" to *Lacan and the Human Sciences* (Alexandre Leupin, ed.; Lincoln, NE: University of Nebraska Press, 1991).

TOPOLOGY

This topology emerges in the unpublished *Séminaire IX, L'identification* (1961–1962) as well as in a text read ten years later, *"L'étourdit."*[50] As in mathematics, it is dependent on what Leibniz invented under the name of *analysis situs*, or analysis of position. This branch of topology is concerned not with quantity but only with quality: that is, the relative positions of geometrical beings to one another. As such, this topology makes meaning (= quantity) dependent on structure (= quality), which is its main preoccupation. Needless to say, this insistence on quality permits at the same time its formalization and its total transmissibility.

In this new formalization, Lacan uses tori (see Fig. 1–8). Lacan foresaw the usefulness of this geometrical entity as early as 1953.[51] A torus is a cylinder joined at its two extremities (a tire's air chamber is a good example). What interests Lacan, again, is that the torus defines two voids: an internal one inside the "tire" itself, and an external one in the center of the shape; these voids point to a lack, an absence, the always missing *o* object or even death or the death instinct:

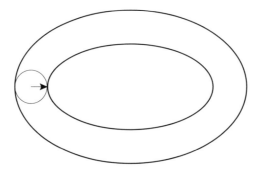

Figure 1–8. A torus.

---

50. *Autres écrits*, p. 469 ff.
51. See for example *Écrits*, pp. 320–321.

We can use the concept of torus's air chamber to articulate desire and request: circles inside the torus's volume will represent requests, and empty ones, inscribed on the torus's circumference and defining its central void, desire. The crossings of these circles define the different objects where the subject tries to tie together request and his desire, to substitute the lost *o* object (see Fig. 1–9):[52]

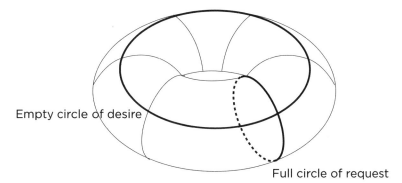

Figure 1–9. Inscription of desire and request on a torus, according to Pierre Scriabine.

The torus can also help us conceive the dynamics of request. Let's begin the count of the objects by an *o* object, noted *n*-1 to manifest its loss (see Fig. 1–10). The object *n* will take its place, but, by its alienating essence (it cannot represent desire adequately, but can be said to

52. From Pierre Scriabine, "Les figures de topologie," in *Qui sont vos psychanalystes?*, J.-A. Miller, ed., p. 401 and also Lacan comment on the void: "A torus has a central or circular void only for somebody who looks at it as an object, not for somebody who is the subject of the torus." "L'Etourdit," *Autres écrits*, p. 485.

remember the loss of the originary object by signifying and veiling it at the same time), it will provoke request to spiral and flee in an endless series of substitutive objects:[53]

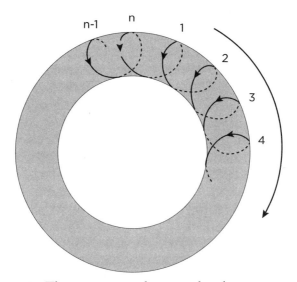

Figure 1–10. The repetition of request for objects, starting from the lost object. (Therefore, the winding can never be completed by a return to the starting point.)

The torus typology, of course, doesn't account for the whole of the subject. In 1972, therefore, Lacan begins to propose his last description of the subject, where the three orders, Real, Symbolic and Imaginary, will be linked in a new way that goes beyond the intended pun on "heresy" in French. It is the Borromean knot that will allow this operation of linkage; the knot figures in the coat of arms of Saint Charles Borromeus (1538–1584), symbolizing the triple alliance of the three branches of the family.

---

53. *Ibid.*, p. 403. See "L'Étourdit," *Autres écrits*, pp. 486–488.

THE BORROMEAN KNOT

Lacan makes a deliberate effort toward a more rigorous, purer (in the sense of more abstract) representation of human beings, a representation that tries to avoid the trap of graphical analogy, but really *is* the subject's structure: "This topology which is written in projective geometry and the surfaces of *analysis situs* represents the structure itself; it is not to be taken like the optical models in Freud, which are metaphorical."[54] Let us add that each geometrical figure is translatable in an algorithm, and vice versa, as mathematics has it.

The knot between strings is defined by the fact that when one string is cut, all the others are cut loose.[55] By virtue of this property, the three agencies or orders are independently defined as mathematical sets, and, at the same time, cannot be conceived separately: a cut would lead to the dissolution of their relationship. They therefore answer to a specific definition that accounts for their radical differentiation even as they are equal: "The required minimum was that each of these three terms, imaginary, symbolic [. . .], real, would be strictly equal to the two others, so that the play would be level."[56]

This new formalization therefore, allows us a representation of the subject where none of the orders logically prevails: the supremacy of the Symbolic over the Imaginary order is gone, replaced by a strict equivalency. In the subject's Borromean representation, there is no ethical hierarchy between the orders; their ordering is only logical and temporal. Hence, if we apply (by retrospection) the last topology to Lacan's earlier attempts, the symbolic order's supremacy appears as an aporia, an ethical decision that logic does not support and that does not justify the crushing of the Imaginary order. In other words, Lacan's anti-Americanism can be jettisoned without harming the doctrinal core.

---

54. "L'objet de la psychanalyse," *Autres écrits*, p. 219.

55. *Séminaire XX*, p. 112.

56. "Conférences et entretiens dans des universités nord-américaines," *Scilicet* 6–7, p. 40.

Here is a Borromean knot (see Fig. 1–11):[57]

Figure 1–11.

The human psyche will be written in a particular Borromean combination of the three exigencies (see Fig. 1–12):[58]

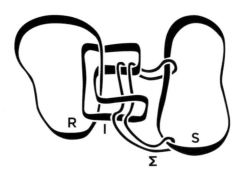

Figure 1–12. The Borromean knot linking the RSI sets.

In this diagram, R = Real, S = Symbolic, Σ = Symptom, I = Imaginary. To hold the three exigencies together, and to preserve the quartenary organization that runs throughout Lacan's work, it is necessary to add

57. *Seminar XX*, English (Fink) p. 125.
58. *Ibid.*, p. 113.

a fourth element: the symptom. The symptom is a signifier; more pre-cisely, a metaphor,[59] unthinkable outside a rhetoric of the unconscious, which produces the individual as a unique combination of the three exigencies: "The symptom is the singular notation of the human dimen-sion," or the last avatar of the *o'* object.[60] It is clear that the three exi-gencies are bound only by a hole in their center: the void is therefore the possibility of linkage itself, repeating in each exigency the lack of the master signifier, the phallus.

For this last topology, Lacan claimed a particular status; stressing its originality, he asserted that it was not a metaphor, a figuration, or an image but a real notation of the human psyche, the real being in-dexed four times in the schema by the void: "I am trying to constitute another geometry, which would deal with the being of the chain. It has never, never been done. This geometry is not imaginary; contrary to the one of triangles, it is real; it is knots of strings."[61]

We need further testing to verify not only the operational and transmissive power of this last drawing of the subject, but also its exac-titude and truth; however, following Nathalie Charraud, what we can say is that there is here "perfect adequation of the mathematical ob-ject with Lacan's statements."[62]

59. *Écrits*, p. 528.
60. "Conférences," p. 56.
61. "Conférences," p. 40.
62. "Mathématiques lacaniennes," in *Qui sont vos psychanalystes?*, J.-A. Miller, ed., p. 386.

2

Epistemology

EPISTEMOLOGY OF SCIENCE, EPISTEMOLOGY OF THE HUMANITIES

The problem of epistemology, until Lacan—and after him, for those who are unaware of his successful attempt—can be sketched in the following terms. On one side stand humanists who are trying to inject metaphors in science, to make of science itself a metaphor. This effort is bound to fail, because science is not a metaphorical discourse, but an exact one that resists metaphorization. On the other side one finds scientists, professional epistemologists, linguists, and logicians who reduce the logical formalization of language to a self-reflexive consciousness that knows itself perfectly, thereby avoiding the recognition of unconscious phenomena and structures. It must be stressed that the vagaries of the subject are not part of the scientist's purview. However, there is no reason to let the humanists metaphorize ad infinitum on this topic. To do so would be akin to a regression to the largely metaphorical science of antiquity, a move rendered rationally illegitimate by our inhabiting a world informed by modern science.[1] What will succeed is not the injection of literature into science, but science's injection into the humanities and, conversely, the injection of rational psychoanalysis into the theory and history of scientific knowledge.

No amount of good will and understanding seems sufficient to bridge this abyss between two opposite sides. The only way out of this impasse is to apply some scientific rigor to human images (metaphor and metonymy, for example) and to the structure of the subject, and to try to grasp the unconscious processes.

This program can be summarized by Lacan's statement: "The subject of the unconscious is the subject of science,"[2] a position that dismisses humanism and reinscribes psychoanalysis in a modern (i.e., scientific) framework. Through psychoanalysis, the questions of the subject and the unconscious may be reintroduced in a general epistemology that includes at the same time both man and his drives and exact science.

Lacan is thus the only thinker to have attempted this construction. Since this is a relatively unbeaten path, I will begin with this general problematic. From the point of view of a lay reader, this is one of the least-known of Lacan's contributions, yet in my opinion it is the most important. Even if psychoanalysis as a cure for psychic ills disappears from the face of the earth, Lacanian epistemology will endure and remain as his crowning achievement. I will therefore devote an ample amount of space to it.

The Language of Mathematics

Lacan begins building a general epistemology by formalizing basic units of common language. In which conditions is such a formalization possible? Mathematics offers here a useful and refined tool, one we can view as a purification and formalization of the basic logical operations implicitly at work in our discourses. Conversely, a mathematical algorithm ultimately makes sense only when it has been retranslated into common language, a process that is automatic for trained mathematicians.

---

1. Of course, this is not to say that we have to stop interpreting the metaphors of the science of Antiquity.

2. *Écrits*, p. 858. This means that other fields will define the subject differently.

Common language and its logic form the insuperable framework of any logical process; mathematical notation is just more economical compared to a complete rephrasing through common language.

To avoid misunderstandings (such as those that provoked the superficial attacks on Lacan by Sokal and Bricmont),[3] a few words of caution on the use of modern logic, mathematics, and topology by Lacan are in order. The ultimate aim of mathematics per se is an exact description of nature. Its use in psychoanalysis obeys another goal. There, it aims at describing the symbolic effects of language on the subject: for Lacan, it is here that the possibility of inscribing part of language in science lies—and as a special operation, because the matter under examination is not a physical phenomenon in the sense of the exact sciences, but in the field of linguistics: "The signified will or will not be thinkable in a scientific way only if the field of the signifier will or will not hold. I add that, through its matter, the field of the signifiers has to be distinguished from any physical field defined by hard science."[4]

In a word, Lacan uses mathematics with all the rigor of a certified mathematician (he sought help from this group as early as 1951),[5] but for a purpose different from the purview admitted by classical mathematics. Summarizing the misunderstanding, he will say to Jean-Michel Vappereau, a specialist in topology: "Mathematicians don't understand what I say, but it is not a reason not to read their works."[6]

Lacan, by his own admission, reduces the language of mathematics to a discourse, which he then submits to the discourse of psychoanalysis.[7]

---

3. Alan Sokal and Jean Bricmont, *Intellectual Impostures*; London: Profile Books, 1988; for the epistemological question of the Lacanian use of mathematics, the best clarification is Jean-Claude Milner's *L'oeuvre claire*, pp. 117–156. For a thorough presentation of Lacan's use of linguistics and algorithms, see Joël Dor, *Introduction to the Reading of Lacan: The Unconscious Structured Like a Language*; New York: Other Press, 1998. This is how Nathalie Charraud summarizes the question: "The use of these mathematical objects is unambiguous: it is not geared towards calculation or as a crutch for would-be demonstrations. Rather, the mathematical objects represent the ultimate reduction of what Freud called "the drying of the Zuydersee (i.e., the understanding of the unconscious)." *Lacan et les Mathématiques*; Paris: Anthropos, 1997, p. 7.

4. "Radiophonie," *Autres écrits*, p. 56.

5. See Elisabeth Roudinesco, *Jacques Lacan*; Paris: Fayard, p. 469 ff.

6. *Ibid.*, p. 475.

7. "L'Étourdit," *Autres écrits*, p. 452.

In brief, the giant step taken by Lacan, and nobody else, is to mathe-matically formalize some parts of common language while including in this formalization the unconscious "structured as a language." Of course, mathematicians and logicians (Frege, Boole, Tarski, and Russell, for example) have long been at work at this endeavor. But their goal is to refine the operation of language as an entirely consistent—that is, self-reflexive and conscious—set, and therefore they cannot include the unconscious, which is inconsistency in itself. Here we can now see Lacan's profound originality, which makes him one of the major think-ers of the twentieth century. In taking this step, Lacan creates a new discipline that can take into account in a rigorous way the symbolic effects of language on man: "So psychoanalysis takes its place—maybe an impossible place—between science and ethics."[8]

If, at the beginnings of his work, Lacan already claims a scientific status for psychoanalysis, this position will evolve. In the end, what remains is a "hope for scientificity,"[9] and the hope that psychoanalysis could be *equal* to science, and therefore distinct from it.[10] Science abol-ishes the unconscious subject, whereas it is the unique preoccupation of psychoanalysis. Hence psychoanalysis will be scientific only up to the point where it abuts against the real and the unconscious. To make unconscious subject the subject of science forces psychoanalysis to take into account the effects of science on the subject and desire, without reducing this subject to science; hence the in-between status claimed for psychoanalysis by Lacan. Such a status questions science because it abolishes the subject (a complete erasure), and questions the humani-ties because they repress the materiality of the subject's symbolic-unconscious dimension.

But we have to consider Lacan's attempt in a larger framework. Let us start from a working definition of modern science, as created by Galileo. Modern science unites two principles that, before its emer-gence, were always separated:

---

8. François Regnault, "Lacan and experience," in *Lacan and the Human Sci-ences*, A. Leupin, ed., p. 44.

9. *Séminaire XI*, p. 23.

10. "Note italienne," *Autres écrits*, p. 310.

1. It is mathematizable (that is, describable in terms of mathematical reasoning);
2. Its algorithms are subjected to an empirical verification (what Karl Popper calls "*falsification*").

You can find one or the other of these characteristics before modern science—the Mayans and the Egyptians had a refined astronomy-astrology, the Greeks an advanced mathematics—but they never applied it to this world. Conversely, the history of technology is full of instrumental progress, but these important tinkerings, like the invention of the windmill, were never raised to the level of a mathematical paradigm; they remained in the field of empirical trial and error without having consequences in theory. And this should not surprise us: an empirical process cannot give birth to a concept by itself. As always, in the beginning was the word: ideas, not sweat, beget ideas. Could it be, then, that the statement "In the beginning was the Word," which we usually ascribe to a religious sphere, also has an epistemological or anthropological value?

I defy anybody to give me a counterexample, one by which a praxis without words would have given birth to a concept. Indeed, a praxis is never without words: it is always already framed by them. Let us take Marx as an example: no amount of toiling by the proletariat can ever give birth to the concept of proletariat. Toiling, unfortunately, does not create ideas, only sweat. The reality is quite the opposite: you need Marx's conceptual and lexical innovation in order for the proletariat to discover itself *as* proletariat. The same reasoning applies to scientific concepts: they cannot emanate from an experiment because the experiment itself is already framed by the scientist in abstract mathematical terms (what Galileo invented and named *experimentum mentis*, mental experiment).

Only Galileo (and after him modern science; that is why Galilean and modern science are treated here as synonyms) unites mathematical speculation with empirical verification. It means that, after him, the words "science" and "experiment" will become homonymous to the terms "science" and "experience" up to the seventeenth century.

We may ask ourselves why the ancients never combined the field of experimentation with a mathematical formalization. That this did not occur has to do with the radical separation between the supralunar world and the sublunar world, which formed the basis of their cosmology. Mathematical precision was the privilege of heaven, the domain of the Gods; the world of Antiquity is a chaos, a *chaosmos*, where chance prevails (a chance that is not submitted to the conjecture of probability calculation). This separation is always respected throughout all civilizations (including the West), up to Galileo; only he had the intuition to submit our world to precision, to think that it was calculable; and concurrently, only he had the idea of introducing variables in the ethereal world of the planets. Of course, the science (a misnomer) of Antiquity compensates for the separation of the sublunar and supralunar world by a mythology that is at work in all cosmologies; it presupposes a mysterious harmony between the macrocosmos and the microcosmos (man).

The science of Antiquity may indeed concern psychoanalysis, but only insofar as it grounds the harmony of the macro- and microcosmos in a sexual mythology, where the harmony of the world is in fact a projection of a supposed harmony of humankind's opposite sexes; in other words, the science of Antiquity (except for parts of its mathematics) is metaphorical, figuring at the same time the symptoms of psychic conflicts and their resolution.

LACAN'S THEORY OF LANGUAGE

The object of psychoanalysis is not nature, not the body, but language. In Lacan's theory (which is, interestingly enough, similar to Stalin's position on the question of language in the only paper he devoted to the question),[11] language is not a superstructure added to an infrastructure. Language is the very matter of thought and of the human world: "The minimum you can grant me about my theory of language is that it is materialist. The signifier is matter that transcends itself in language."[12] The primary signifying matter is what allows, for example,

---

11. Joseph V. Stalin, "Marxism and Problems of Linguistics," published in the June 20, July 4, and August 2, 1950 issues of *Pravda*.

12. *Autres écrits*, p. 209.

the secondary differentiation between infrastructure and superstructure, or the distinction between the master and the slave, or, for that matter, any distinction. In that sense, and Lacan makes the connection himself, his theory of language *is materialism itself*, a radical materialism—much more radical than the Marxist "dialectical materialism." This theory of language is also a realism, in the sense that this epithet acquired during the Middle Ages through the quarrels over universals:[13] for Lacan, as for the medieval realists, statements are, through the signifier that is their indispensable condition of existence, real matter, not names only; the signifier is the matter of our thought processes, conscious or unconscious. Hence, signifiers can evoke something real. On the other hand, at least since Ockham (fourteenth century) and up to his heirs in modern academia, nominalism professes that words describing general categories are but words. As modern nominalism formulates this theory of language, signifiers are but signifiers referring to other signifiers without designating anything as real (a subject, for example). In a sense, nominalism can be conceived as a defense mechanism repressing the real materiality of the signifier, the possibility for a statement to be true or exact. Since the signifier and its consequence, the unconscious, are external to the ego, nominalism can also be seen as a defense by the ego's narcissism against everything that dislodges it from its illusory position of centrality. "To profess that the sign is but a representation (of the thing) is not logical, but political."[14] What is logical is to assert the real materiality of language.

The profoundly embedded realism of the entire Lacanian theory is what makes his bundling with other French postmodern thinkers impossible. For example, Foucault and Derrida, like Stanley Fish in

---

13. "Logical realism (in the medieval sense of the term) is so implied in science that science doesn't even remark on it. Five hundred years of nominalism would be interpreted as a resistance and would evaporate if some political conditions would not unite those who survive only by professing that the signs are but a representation" (*Ibid.*, p. 327). However, this has to be corrected by the affirmation (*Ibid.*, p. 351) that modern science and psychoanalysis don't apply logical realism to ideas, but to nature and linguistic matter respectively. In the last analysis, therefore, medieval realism is homonymous to the realism of modern science.

14. *Ibid.*, p. 328.

America, are unreconstructed nominalists who would be shocked by a declaration like this one made by Lacan: "It is false to say that interpretation is open to all meanings, under the pretext that interpretation is but a liaison from a signifier to a signifier; this liaison is madness. It is absolutely absurd to say that all interpretations are possible."[15] This relates specifically to psychoanalytical interpretation. Interpretations satisfying themselves with an assessment of the signifier only (therefore excluding any real meaning) result as a matter of course in absolute relativism, since it is true that no signifier is privileged over another, that they derive their values from a differential comparison to each other. Quite to the contrary, for psychoanalysis, there is, for each individual, a sublated signifier of his or her desire: an unconscious *o* object, a "master-signifier,"[16] a something that does not participate in the signifying chain and motivates its meaning.

Closely linked with Lacan's realism (against nominalism and idealism) are two synonymous statements he repeats over and over: "There is no metalanguage" and "There is no Other of the Other," as in "There is no Other of the Other (as a matter of fact), neither a truth of truth (by rights)."[17] If the structure of language encompasses the totality of human reality, if it is real, then there is nothing beyond it. You cannot build a metalanguage to examine language itself: it too would obey the structure of language. This is true of mathematics too, since its operation has to be explained in common language. In other words, it is not possible to say the truth about truth, since truth is grounded in the fact that it is spoken. A hypothetical metalanguage would not master the description of language itself: both exhibit the same incompleteness, both lay bare the split of the subject, with this part called the unconscious escaping words. Hence a metalanguage is a symptom for an illu-

---

15. *Séminaire XI*, pp. 225–226. See also: "There is only one interpretation that is correct" (*Autres écrits*, p. 136). I add: not all interpretations are born equal. See also below for the Lacanian definition of the signifier.

16. The expression "master-signifier," frequently used by Lacan to designate the phallus or the *o* object, has, from the point of view of linguistics, no sense. For Saussurean linguistics, all signifiers are of equal, negative, and differential value. As such, the concept of "master-signifier" makes clear how much Lacan's theory goes beyond linguistics in order to include a Real in the operations of language.

17. "Discours à l'école freudienne de Paris," *Autres écrits*, p. 265.

sion of mastery that in fact repeats the illusion of logical positivism (that there is an autonomous ego fully and reflexively conscious of itself). Translated to academic jargon, this position can be schematized as the proposition that we cannot but produce "interpretations of interpretations" ad infinitum, a proposition whose validity Lacan refutes both in science and humanities.

"There is no Other of the Other" is a rephrasing of "There is no metalanguage"; it means that, whatever our wishes, we cannot go beyond the Symbolic order to try to grasp its structure: the Symbolic order (language) can be enlightened only by itself. There is no infinite regression from one descriptive language to another, it all ends up in the Symbolic order itself.

If the latter is in fact the cause of castration (by prohibiting desire), "There is no Other of the Other" means that, sooner or later, the signifier inevitably will abut against castration. The attempt at creating a metalanguage, an illusory "Other of the Other," can thus only mean a repression, an avoidance of castration, or a sublimation.

In this context, we have to avoid a number of confusions, the main one being between animal code and human language. Yes, whales communicate, but it is through a code, that is, a system of signs where each sign has one and only one meaning—that is, not a language, which is equivocal. A whale can certainly say to another whale "I love you" (or more likely, "I want to copulate with you in order for the species to perpetuate itself"). It can indicate where it is, or signal danger and other situations to other whales. But it cannot say "I hate you" when those words mean the opposite, whereas we humans do it all the time because we use an equivocal language, not a univocal code. And also, so far as I know, there is no congress of whales deep in the sea to examine the nature of their codes, whereas linguistic colloquia are somewhat frequent in our human sphere. In other words, because animal codes don't exhibit the distinction between signifier and signified, the signs they emit have but one meaning; conversely, the distinction between the signifier and the signified is what characterizes human language and makes it ambiguous and equivocal.

The first formalization and differentiation between signifier and signified was the result of Ferdinand de Saussure's work around the turn of the twentieth century. This very distinction heralded the era of scientific linguistics. In the *Course in General Linguistics*, Saussure offers us the first possibility of a mathematization of common language, with his formula of the sign:

$\frac{s}{S}$ = s', where
s = signified (any concept, or representation, or signification)
S = signifier (any linguistic object)
s' = meaning or statement

The result of the operation and relation between signified and signifier (what ultimately will lead us to meaning) is called *sign*, and Saussure makes a fascinating statement: "As far as *sign* is concerned, if we satisfied ourselves with this substantive, it is because we don't know by what we could replace it: common language doesn't suggest any other."[18]

For Saussure, the operation that produces meaning has no name, and it cannot be named: it is not representable. For an analytic ear, this can mean only one thing: it is unconscious. Meaning exists and is real, but remains for the most part beyond any representation. We can affirm that Saussure intuited the existence of the unconscious as the disappearing key to meaning; the existence of the *Anagrams* published by Jean Starobinski proves it.[19] Saussure devoted the better part of his later years not to perfecting the science he had founded, but to a search for a secret, unpronounced sentence that would have been the key to unlock the deep meaning of Latin poetry up to the nineteenth century. Hence Lacan can claim that the "sliding of the signified under the signifier [. . .] always in action (in an unconscious way) in discourse" did not escape Saussure.[20] In other words, after having declared the arbitrariness of the sign, or more exactly the arbitrariness of the link between signifier and signified (a fact easily demonstrated by the existence of different languages), Saussure spends three years (1906–1909) of his life trying to "remotivate" the sign, to show that it was indeed not arbitrarily tied to meaning. He thinks he will find this motivation in a secret word containing the meaning, the key, of certain Latin poems.

---

18. *Cours de linguistique générale*, Tullio di Mauro, ed.; Paris: Payot, 1972 (my translation), pp. 99–100.

19. Jean Starobinski, *Les mots sous les mots. Les Anagrammes de Ferdinand de Saussure*; Paris: Gallimard, 1971, where Starobinski speaks of "verbal latency."

20. *Écrits*, p. 511.

The quest won't (and couldn't) be successful. It would have been a success only if Saussure had had access to the notion of the Freudian unconscious. Similarly, Freud could have built a successful formalization of his discovery only if he had had access to Saussurean linguistics.

Half a century later, Lacan takes the Saussurean writing literally,[21] as an operation on the sign. He combines Freud's discovery of the unconscious and Saussure's scientific linguistics. Furthermore, by relying on the *Anagrams*, Lacan shows that the sign in human language is indeed motivated, as Saussure secretely believed (the *Anagrams* were notes not destined for publication). Saussure's secret intuition is correct, only his method is flawed, and for historical reasons, since he had no access to Freud's theory.

However, the motivation of the sign is bound to escape the observations of a typical linguistics, since linguistics deals with representations by limiting itself to signifiers and signifieds: "The unconscious may be the condition of linguistics. But the latter cannot grasp the former at all."[22] The motivation of the sign escapes representation: it is unconscious. Hence linguistics as practiced by Lacan, who includes the unconscious in its problematic, will be baptized by him "linguistery": "What I call linguistery demands psychoanalysis as its condition. I will add that there is no other linguistics than linguistery, which doesn't mean that psychoanalysis is the whole of linguistics."[23]

Since psychoanalysis takes into account the subject of the unconscious through linguistic structures, its object is not language as it is traditionally dealt with in linguistics, but a broader, different object that Lacan calls *lalangue*,[24] "thetongue," of which language is only a part.

In fact, in a very late paper (1975), Lacan still reduces the anchoring of psychoanalysis in science to the signifier as distinct from the signified. At the same time, a new light could be thrown on science, inasmuch as science ultimately depends on common language: "Linguistics grounded its object by isolating it under the name of

---

21. There is thus a profound difference between taking writing according to the letter—seriously, as a realism—and literalism, which is another name for the idolization of the signifier.

22. "Radiophonie," *Autres écrits*, p. 410.

23. *Ornicar?* 17–18, 1979, p. 7.

24. See for example "Télévision," *Autres écrits*, p. 514.

signifier. It is the only point where psychoanalytical discourse has to anchor itself in science, but, if the unconscious testifies for a real that is its own, it is, inversely, our chance to elucidate how language conveys, through numbers, the real on which science is elaborated."[25]

In repeating Saussure's algorithm, Lacan corrects it. Saussure made an error in putting the signified first; in fact we always accede to the signified or signification through signifiers. This is how Lacan indicates the "primacy of the signifier" (see Fig. 2–1):

$$\frac{S}{s} = \acute{s}$$

Figure 2–1. Saussure's formula of the sign as reordered by Lacan.

But that is not the only infidelity Lacan commits toward Saussure. Saussure defines the signifier as a negative and differential value because it acquires a signified and a meaning only in comparison with all the other signifiers: it has no value in and by itself. Lacan's definition of the signifier is grounded on Saussure, but extends it: "Our definition of the signifier is the following (there is no other definition): a signifier is what represents the subject for another signifier."[26] This means that Saussure's linguistic doctrine has to be completed by the inclusion of the unconscious, and that psychoanalysis supersedes linguistics, becoming a Lacanian linguistery by reintroducing the subject in the equation. In 1970, Lacan repeats the definition: "The signifier represents a subject, according to Lacan (not a signified), for an other signifier (which means not for an other subject)."[27] Let me give two examples: the signifier Alexandre (not the person, not the body, but how she conceives me) represents my subject for the signifier Kate (not the person, not the body, but how she conceives herself). Or, during the cure,

---

25. "Introduction to the German Edition of the Écrits," *Scilicet* 5, p. 17.

26. *Écrits*, p. 819.

27. "Radiophonie," *Autres écrits*, p. 413. For example, your proper name represents you as subject for another proper name (the person you address) and vice versa.

the analysand represents himself as subject, not for the analyst's unconscious or person, but for the analyst's name, which he has incorporated through transference.

Here again, we have to avoid the idolatry of literalism: the bar between the signifier and the signified in the corrected formula of the sign in Fig. 2–1 should be taken neither as an intuition of proportion nor as a fraction bar: "The bar through which Saussure notes the relative impossibility for the signifier to go to the signified has nothing to do with the Euclidian proportion bar."[28] Indeed, since there is no relationship of the signifier to itself, this means that you cannot consider the bar as a fraction bar (such a literalism would be akin to a delirious abuse or misuse, Lacan says);[29] it is a border as conceived by topology. The bar is a real border between the complete and closed set of signifiers and the complete and closed set of signifieds belonging to any language. The bar is the limit and the relation, the operation that produces meaning. (See Appendix I for more details.)

Let me now give a concrete illustration of the functioning of the sign's formula. As a professor at a college, you write an e-mail to your chairperson proposing changes in your department, aimed at improving its operation. In order to write the e-mail, you have to make use of the computer code deep in the machine. This code can be reduced to a series of numbers { 0, 1 } and their combinations. The code is the mere digitalization of the basic units of any human language on the face of the earth since the beginning of speech, and it can produce not only letters, but sentences, messages, books, pictures, games, movies, indeed entire worlds of representations: it is the set of signifiers. Not only can the code function by itself, like a machine, but you are aware neither of its existence nor of its working process. (As a strict analogy, you don't need to know grammar and linguistics in order to utter a sentence.) However, at this point, we cannot say that the code can be assimilated to the symbolic-unconscious order: it lacks the human dimension of the unconscious, which is introduced only when you use the code to issue

---

28. *Autres écrits*, p. 400. See also the remarks in *Séminaire XI*, pp. 224–225.

29. *Ibid.*, p. 68. "The bar cannot be manipulated in a fractional transformation because the signifier cannot have a relationship with itself" (*Séminaire XI*, p. 224). Nominalism presupposes this relationship and puts it at the center of its inquiry, but according to Lacan, it is a "mad relationship" (*ibid.*, p. 225), inasmuch as nominalism, like psychosis, evacuates real meaning.

and send a statement. Were the computer to be endowed with an un-conscious, the ultimate stage of artificial intelligence would have been reached, and the machine would be human. In any case, the code, as well as its symbolic-unconscious motivation, will both remain hidden from you when you use it.

To write your e-mail, you borrow and isolate specific elements of the set of signifiers. These will create a representation for you, the signifieds of your e-mail, which we summarize as "improving the de-partment's operation." When the e-mail is sent, your chairperson looks at the signifiers, and, overcoming the bar that separates signifiers from signifieds,[30] attributes signification to your message: "improving the de-partment's operation." At the level of imaginary *signification*, the con-tent of the message is already ambiguous for you and for its recipient as well. Your conscious intention in sending the e-mail may be to bother your chairperson whom you find impossible to deal with; he or she, when he or she receives the message, may also attribute that significa-tion to it, or even a broader range of contents.

So far, the real *meaning* of your e-mail remains obscure to you: in order to elucidate the "why" of your enunciation, we have to know more about you; maybe you didn't sleep enough and woke up in an aggres-sive mood, or, it is difficult for you to tolerate any kind of institutional authority, or, you are in love with your chairperson and you want to call his or her attention to you. In a mirror fashion, the e-mail may cre-ate a broad range of unconscious meanings for your recipient: love, hate, fear that you want to unseat him or her from his/her lofty position as chairperson. In any case, between the signifiers and the signifieds, there is a gap, which the reader or the psychoanalyst has to cross over in order to discover both the signification and the meaning of the statement.

The bar distinguishing the signifier and the signified differentiates the Symbolic and the Imaginary orders. For Lacan, the distinction is so important because it suffices to constitute the field of scientific psy-choanalysis: "From the time the symbolic and imaginary orders have been distinguished, our science and its field have been born."[31]

---

30. "The crossing over of the bar sets up the signification's emergence." *Écrits*, p. 515.

31. "La psychanalyse, raison d'un échec," *Autres écrits*, p. 349.

Moreover, an erasure of the differentiation between signifier and signified, the folding of the materiality, Otherness and structure of the unconscious order into single signs has consequences for applied psychoanalysis (a cure). As Lacan enumerates them,[32] to collapse the two levels is to presume that there are only signifieds and significations in a human world and to fall prey to the obscurantism of the imaginary order. It also amounts to reinforcing a kind of psychic orthopedics, by adhering to an imaginary normative psychology, since only the other, not the Other, is at hand; it is to take seriously the neurotic alibi, which incarnates its defenses in signifieds in order not to grasp the truth of their meaning, which can be accessible only through signifiers. In brief, it amounts to reinforcing the imaginary defenses the ego opposes to the Symbolic order and the unconscious.

Through the distinction of the signifer and the signified, reality and the Real order will be differentiated: "The Real order is distinct from reality; it doesn't mean this Real order is unknowable, it means that it is demonstrable. This way of inquiry is free of any form of idealism."[33] Hence, we can add another dimension to Lacan's theory: its realism pits it not only against medieval and modern nominalism, but against philosophical idealism as well. Freud had already remarked on the opposition between idealism and psychoanalysis:[34] for the founder of psychoanalysis, Kant's a priori of mental categories, through which we are supposed to see the world, are projections of the psyche. Hence "reality," the "reality of the world" are projections too, also in the geometrical sense.

Lacan developed the status of reality in an ad lib improvisation in front of one of his students, who took notes.[35] He noted that absolute awakening would be equivalent to death. Hence we always dream: at night, in order to go on sleeping, we dream in order not to wake up, therefore sustaining the very life of our bodies (sleep deprivation would mean death). Inasmuch as our desire works during the day too, we never wake up, we never stop dreaming. This does not mean that Lacan agrees

---

32. "La psychanalyse vraie, et la fausse," *Autres écrits*, p. 168.

33. "Radiophonie," *Autres écrits*, p. 60. This is consistent with the materialism of Lacanian theory.

34. In a manuscript note collected in GW XXII, p. 132.

35. Catherine Millot, "Désir de mort, rêve et réveil," in *L'Ane 3*, 1981, p. 3.

with Eastern mysticism, however; for him, life is not a dream, and the function of our daydreaming is to protect the real core of our desire.

Lacan further develops the formula of the sign, which is now no longer Saussurean, but Lacanian (see Fig. 2–2):[36]

$$f(S)\frac{I}{s}$$

Figure 2–2.

Let us develop this to Fig. 2–3:

$$f\left(\frac{S}{s}\right) = f(S) \cdot \frac{I}{s}$$

Figure 2–3.

"I" is an imaginary identity in mathematics; here it is used to denote a projection or identification, an *o* object.

With a concrete example (a sentence that all of us have uttered at some point; see Fig. 2–4), the formula will become clearer:

$$\frac{f(\text{I love you})}{s = \text{what it means for } me} = f(\text{I love you}) \cdot \frac{I}{s = \text{what it means for } you}$$

Figure 2–4.

The left-hand side of the equation is the side of the speaker, the right-hand the side of the auditor. This will apply to any and all the algorithms

---

36. *Écrits*, p. 515.

Lacan intersperses in his work, when they describe an enunciation: the first side describes a speech act, the second the way it is received. The two sides may be the same person; in fact they often are, if we accept that narcissism (= I love myself) is the primary form of love. The sign = is the result of the first transformation, the passage from the speaker to the auditor. Hence the statement creates in the auditor an image, a signifier (I), to which, overcoming the bar of signification, he or she will attribute a signified.

Before going on to the extension of this seminal algorithm to metaphor and metonymy, let us note that the formula of meaning can be easily reinscribed within the schema L', and that, as we did with the schema, we can develop each agency with approximate synonyms (see Fig. 2–5):

As far as the signified is concerned, Lacan adds a new twist; first, we have to distinguish between signification and meaning. Here,

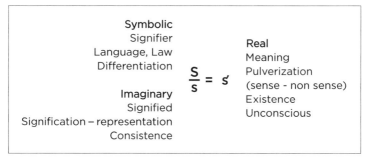

Figure 2–5. Formula of the sign with R, S, I sets.

signification is always representable—we can form an image of it—and as such it is supported by the Imaginary. Hence, what we call reality, as opposed to the Real, is always a fictional image: idealism and nominalism are both trapped here in thinking that the reality of signification is indeed equal to the Real order of meaning. By virtue of its evidence for us, these images of reality have a certain consistence. We know what objects we request in reality.

On the contrary, meaning is on the side of the Real. That is, meaning (the truth of our desire) is always partially or entirely buried in our unconscious. Furthermore, if the Symbolic and the Imaginary (difference and signification) are always characterized by an aspect that is shared with others, a social dimension, truth is singular to each individual. That is in essence the big difference between the unconscious of Freud and Lacan and the archetypes of Jung. Jung in fact put the Freudian edifice upside down when he supposed that archetypes (symbols, mythologies, stories shared by such and such society) are located in the unconscious. The fact that they are common to a group of individuals, in fact, is enough to mark them as belonging either to the Symbolic or the Imaginary.

Furthermore, if meaning and truth escape representation, partially or in toto, it means that they are never entirely decidable; therefore, they are submitted to a certain pulverization, they escape the grasp of representation: meaning can easily invert itself in meaninglessness, sense into nonsense. The core of our being is partially obscured, and this is why we very often cannot decide what it is we really wish. The pulverization of the Real leads to our uncertainty.

Let us now follow Lacan when he applies the general algorithm of the sign to the proper name (see Fig. 2–6):[37]

$$\frac{-1}{s} = \varsigma \qquad \varsigma = \sqrt{-1}$$

Figure 2–6.

Why is the signifier of the proper name noted as "–1"? Because it designates in itself an absolutely singular being: the unconscious of one individual. As such, it has to be subtracted from the closed and complete set of the signifiers, which cannot designate a singularity since their significations depend on their relative opposition to each other (simple Saussurean definition of the signifier). This –1 is what (phallus, master signifier, lost o object) the signifying chain does not accommodate among its links: "I strive to make you conceive the subject as rejected from the signifying chain, which, by the same token, is constituted as primordial repressed material."[38]

It is also another, minimalist way to note castration: as individuals, we desire, but this singular desire cannot be fully and satisfactorily

---

37. *Écrits*, p. 819
38. *Autres écrits*, p. 181.

expressed by any signifier. The signifier of desire is always inadequate; desire is always beyond its realization.

This notation of the proper name describes adequately the result of an operation that can demonstrate an existence (of the unconscious) but, as it leads to the imaginary number, cannot affirm exactly what is the content of this unconscious: "The −I signifier is not utterable, but its operation is, for this operation emerges each time a proper name is pronounced. Its signified equals its signification."[39]

Rhetorical Processes of the Dream Work

In *The Interpretation of Dreams*, published in 1900, Freud identified two essential processes of the dream work, the *Verdichtung* (condensation) and the *Verschiebung* (displacement). As often is the case in his work, these processes are explained through an energetic economy that ultimately harks back to nineteenth-century thermodynamics. Lacan repositions these processes where they belong, which is in the realms of linguistics and rhetoric. Even if the whole arsenal of the figures of classical rhetoric are at one point used by the unconscious, Freud's theory leads Lacan to insist on condensation and displacement as rhetorical figures. Condensation becomes metaphor, and displacement metonymy. Furthermore, Lacan opposes them in their functions: metaphor, by substituting one signifier for another, will mask its first signifier and therefore be at the service of repression; metonymy, by keeping intact a concrete connection to its first signifier, will be the mark of a desire.[40] Lastly, he will provide a mathematical formalization of the two rhetorical processes (see Fig. 2–7).

Here is how the formula of metonymy reads:[41]

$$f(S...S')S \cong S(\,-\,)s$$

Figure 2–7.

---

39. *Ecrits*, p. 819.
40. *Écrits*, pp. 511 and 528.
41. *Ibid.*, p. 515. The (−) is not a division bar; it is the bar separating the signifier from the signified; see Appendix I.

The metonymical connection is indicated by the dots: ". . .". The passage from the speaker to the auditor (the result of the first transformation) is noted here by a ≅, which doesn't indicate an equality, but a congruence: that is, the result of the first operation. The (−) indicates the absence of being operated by the metonymy; it connects us to the ultimate object of our desire, which in psychoanalysis is the mother, but only in an incomplete, partial way. In this regard, our objects of love are always synecdoches, fetishes, partial objects representing a whole that remains forever out of our grasp. An example will clarify the functioning of metonymy. I take it from the Proverbs' exhortations to marital fidelity: "Let her breasts satisfy thee at all times" (5:19):

f (first signifier . . . second signifier) first signifier = First signifier (−)
signified
f (breasts . . . the whole body of your wife) breasts = breasts (−)
femininity

We can note in passing that Proverbs here gives a prescription, not only to avoid other women's breasts, to limit satisfaction to one woman, but also, more profoundly, to find satisfaction in the sexual relationship. The fact that a godly prescription is needed here lets us suspect that a whole satisfaction, a completeness reached through sexual union, is nothing but unattainable.

Now, here is the algorithm of the metaphor (see Fig. 2–8):[42]

$$f\left(\frac{S'}{S}\right) S \cong S(+)s$$

Figure 2–8.

Or, to write out Fig. 2–8 in the terms we have been using:

$$f\frac{\text{(Second signifier)}}{\text{(First signifier)}} \text{ First signifier} \cong \text{First signifier } (+) \textit{ signified}$$

---

42. *Ibid.* The (+) indicates the overcoming of the bar (−), which allows both the destinator and the destinatee to let signification emerge.

On the side of the speaker, a second signifier has been substituted for a first one. The operation of substitution affects the first signifier—it hides it. However, it stays metonymically connected to the signifying chain: that is why it is repeated. Then it reappears on the side of the auditor, who adds its signified by overcoming (+) the bar between signifier and signified. Again, another example, also drawn from the Bible, should make things clear: it is the Lord's promise of a progeny to Abraham: "So shall thy seed be" (Gen 15:5):

$$f\frac{(\text{Seed of Abraham})}{(\text{Abraham})}\text{Abraham} \cong \text{Abraham} (+) \text{Isaac and his descendants}$$

The results obtained by these formalizations are the following: the vagueness of the literary use of such terms as metaphor and metonymy is relegated to the shop of antiquated accessories; in particular, the analogical mode of thinking that surfaces in the theories and practices of metaphor is repudiated. Moreover, the rigorous application of algorithms allows for the uncovering, in each case (and the examples could be multiplied ad infinitum), of a truth that is only half said by the rhetorical figures. My example of metonymy leads to the laying bare of a certain anxiety about femininity, more precisely about the possibility of a femininity to be coupled to masculinity. We have here a hint of the absence of sexual rapport, which is one of the major themes of the Bible. In the case of this metaphor, the doubt about real paternity leads to the necessary affirmation of this paternity in the Symbolic order: fatherhood exists only through a naming act. The fact that God has to take care of it should lead us to meditate about the paternal function (He is here the irruption of the signifier, the principle of paternity that names the father, that produces the Name-of-the-Father). Moreover, the fact that paternity is a metaphor makes us grasp its essentially fictional character. Until today, when real fatherhood can be tested with DNA, we had to follow the Latin dictum, *Mater semper certa, parter semper incertum*; in other words, there is incontrovertible empirical evidence for maternity, but paternity is always a question mark that only a symbolic declaration of fatherhood can answer. The metaphor of the male sperm as a "seed" has the same effect: it inscribes paternity in nature, therefore repressing the cultural aspect of any specific fatherhood as it existed before DNA testing (that is, for almost the entire duration of human history).

In Lacan's theory, there is a signifier that will combine the Freudian condensation (metonymy) and displacement (metaphor). As a metonymy, the phallus will embody, in a visible fashion, desire; but, since it assigns an imaginary goal to desire (therefore alienating it), it also functions as a metaphor: a displacement of the desire's insatiable nature: "The most serious reality (the phallus), and even for humankind the only serious one, if we consider the phallus's role as sustaining the metonymy of humankind's desire, can be grasped only in the metaphor."[43]

A UNIFIED EPISTEMOLOGY

Once a minimum of mathematical formalization of language is assured, we have the means to put sciences and humanities on the same level, and to compare them and try to define their relationship. So far, only psychoanalysis allows us to unify the fields of humanities and sciences. This could very well mean that psychoanalysis has to claim for itself something outrageous: a special status regarding science *and* humanities, an in-between position from which everything has to be reevaluated.

Lacan doesn't condone the view that opposes exactitude (the result of a scientific operation) and truth and considers them mutually exclusive. The classical division that separates the so-called "sciences" from the so-called "arts" in common discourse (we have only to think of our own academic colleges) is not valid. In this view, psychoanalysis would be doomed to remain attached to the arts and confined to the status of an art of interpretation, a hermeneutic of meaning. It would be incapable of determining itself as a science or of striving for the status of one. By contrast, the thrust of Lacanian thought is geared toward establishing a rational compatibility between science and truth by opening their apparent borders without, however, confusing them. And here is where Lacan's profound originality and brilliance reside; this is the answer he gave to François Georgin, when asked about the relation between sciences and humanities:

---

43. *Écrits*, p. 892.

QUESTION VI: *In what sense are science and truth incompatible?*
ANSWER: Incompatible. A cutely chosen word that would allow us to answer by the snub it deserves: but yes, but yes, they sympathize.
They suffer together, one from another and vice versa: it is the truth.
But what you want to say, if I understand you well, is that truth and knowledge are not complementary, that they don't make a whole.
Excuse me: it is not a question that I ask myself. Since there is no whole, nothing is whole.[44]

As we see, the question of the articulation of science and truth is tackled from the angle of a lack, an impossibility of totalization, from which their compatibility (not their complementarity, which would suppose a completeness) has to be envisioned.

On one hand, in the field of exact sciences, Lacan points out that inside the closed system of a given science some fundamental propositions are not demonstrable: it is impossible to prove either their falsity or their accuracy. He follows here the Austrian mathematician Kurt Gödel and his demonstration of the theorems of incompleteness. There is an infinite number of theorems whose validity cannot be proven or disproven. In order to validate this kind of theorem, which often constitutes the basis of reasoning, the scientist has to resort either to an arbitrary decision (to transform the theorem into an aporia) or to another scientific system (which puts into question the rational unity of his own field and shows that this field cannot aspire to a totalization): "A system defined as of the order of arithmetic gains the possibility of separating exactitude and falsehood in its own field only by confirming its incompleteness and by being compelled to resort to indemonstrable formulas that are verified only elsewhere."[45] Such interventions demonstrate that the subject of science cannot be envisioned as complete or whole but is open to an arbitrary decision or divided by the ultimate nonunity of its field. In other words, the impossibility of completeness underlines the fact that the subject of science cannot be "sutured" (that is, be determined, and thus closed, in an entirely rational fashion): "[Modern logic] is without doubt the strictly determined

44. "Radiophonie," *Autres écrits*, p. 440.
45. *Ibid.*, p. 427.

consequence of an attempt at suturing the subject of science, and Gödel's last theorem proves that this attempt fails; it means that this subject remains the correlative of science but an antinomic correlative, since science is defined by the impossibility of suturing the subject."[46] Consequently, there is a hole in the field of science that prevents its rational totalization. The theorem of incompleteness not only makes mathematics incomplete in principle, it makes the scientific totalization of the subject of science (of the unconscious) impossible.

On the other hand, in the fields of the humanities, the function of the hole is taken up by the unconscious; the two incompletenesses become figures of one another: "The rifts of the unconscious show [the structure of scientific incompleteness] when they verify it by losses that have to be similarly defined."[47] This linking of the impossibility of scientific suture and the incompleteness of truth is Lacan's central contribution to epistemology.

Conjecture itself does not lead to ineffability or imprecision, insofar as it is susceptible of a calculation of probabilities; therefore, the necessity of a conjecture about the unconscious "doesn't preclude rigor"[48] and so may be approached with a certain degree of exactitude. The symmetry and compatibility of the discourses of sciences and conjecture thus established render their classical opposition obsolete: "The opposition between exact sciences and conjectural ones can no longer be sustained if the conjecture is susceptible of an exact calculation (probability) and if exactitude is grounded only in a formalism that separates axioms and laws of the grouping of symbols."[49]

In fact, the "conjectural sciences," formerly known as humanities or social sciences, are in themselves part of modern science, but only if they leave their analogical reasoning at the door and include the unconscious in their purview. An example will clarify this: life insurance is but a rigorous conjecture, a calculation of the probability of risk; opinion polls would furnish another example. Both are a calculation (on the side of science or the exactitude of probability) made to assess

---

46. *Écrits*, p. 861.
47. *Ibid.*
48. *Ibid.*, p. 286.
49. *Ibid.*, p. 863.

a desire: in one case, to provide for your loved ones, on the other, to be elected or stay popular, and so on.[50]

By now, the provocative statement "There is no science of man"[51] or, to put it another way, there are no Human sciences can be elucidated. It is another synonym for "there is no metalanguage," which Lacan formulates thus: "There is no science of man, because the man of science doesn't exist, only its subject."[52] Therefore, the appellation "human sciences" is rejected by Lacan: it is for him "a call to servitude": any science that considers man as its object, instead of tackling the subject of science as envisioned by psychoanalysis, is bound to reinforce a slavery to fantasy. Lacan gives a good example of this servitude in psychology, when it serves corporate purposes, often to the detriment of a less narrow purpose. This means also that psychoanalysis cannot be "applied," except as a treatment of specific mental pain in individual cases. Nor can other sciences (for example linguistics or mathematics) be applied to psychoanalysis. Applications presuppose a strict separation between the observing subject and object. Such a methodological hypothesis is supported neither by modern science, where experiments are mental constructs that build (hence modify) their objects, nor by psychoanalysis, where the analyst's unconscious is implied in the transference. Any kind of objectivation is impossible, because the observing subject is always implied in its objects. Therefore, for Lacan, the term "applied psychoanalysis" designates only the cure. It may even be called a misnomer. It should be called involved psychoanalysis, since both patient and analyst are implicated in the process of the cure. The interpretations of Michelangelo, President Schreber, and Jensen's *Gradiva*, by Freud, as well as Lacan's own examples, like Edgar Allan Poe, Paul Claudel, Marguerite Duras, Shakespeare, and James Joyce, thus function more as mental cases destined to advance theoretical psychoanalysis than as objects separated from the observer. In other words, psychoanalysis is not applied to these objects: to the contrary, they enlighten the analytical field.

---

50. "The traduction of 'man is mortal' in scientific discourse is life insurance. Death, in scientific discourse, is a matter of a probability calculation." "L'Étourdit," *Autres écrits*, p. 475.

51. See *Écrits*, p. 859.

52. *Ibid.*

If psychoanalysis cannot be conceived outside the field of modern science, this science, in turn, is unthinkable without psychoanalysis, which points out the lack of suture of the subject: "Truth makes a hole in science."[53] Therefore: "Psychoanalysis is privileged in the sense that in it symbolism is reduced to the effect of truth which, whether extracted or not from its pathetical forms, is isolated in its knot as the counterpart without which nothing can be conceived about science."[54]

The compatibility of science (exactitude) and conjecture (truth) points to a relationship of inclusion/exclusion. To figure it out, Lacan again draws upon the Möbius strip.[55] Here we go from the Möbian structure of the subject[56] to a much broader generalization concerning the status of knowledge in a world (ours) living after the Galilean revolution.

Let us first cut a strip of paper with one face bearing the inscription "truth" (as referring to conjectural sciences) and the opposite face, "exactitude" (as referring to mathematizable sciences) (see Fig. 2–9):

Figure 2–9.

Let us now imagine a homunculus walking on either one of these faces. From his point of view, the surface he is walking on is incompatible with the other side: in order to change surfaces, he would have to leave one side. In other words, he is under the impression that the fields of sciences and arts are, by an external prescription, heterogeneous. Moreover, he has to assume that each of the surfaces has a finite horizon, a limit and a direction (the strip is orientable). He therefore lives with the classical and reassuring opposition between arts and sciences, apparently knowing where he goes.

53. *Ibid.*, p. 234.
54. *Ibid.*, p. 724.
55. *Ibid.*, p. 553.
56. See Chapter II.

In order to show how exactitude and truth may be compatible, let us now make a half-twist in the strip and then glue its two extremities together (Fig. 2–10). The result is a Möbius strip:

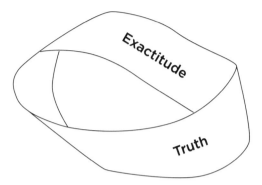

Figure 2–10.

Our homunculus's situation has completely changed. While he still believes that he is walking toward a horizon (that his progress has a direction), he is in fact circling the strip (a Möbius strip is not orientable and has but one surface). Moreover, although he still believes that arts and sciences are opposed, in fact they are now inscribed on the same side of the strip, since a Möbius strip has only one surface and one side. In other words, the opposition between the two sides is no longer external; it is internal to the structure. The subject of science is at the same time in and out of both truth and exactitude.[57]

This figuration could give the impression that the modern subject is enclosed in a vicious repetition, a kind of Nietzschean eternal return of the same, the more so when we read such assumptions in Lacan himself: "Our return to Freud has a totally different meaning, because it is deduced from the topology of the subject, which is elucidated only by a second turn on itself. All of topology has to be repeated on another surface in order to close what it encompasses."[58]

---

57. "If we may say so, the subject is in an internal exclusion to its object." *Écrits*, p. 861.

58. *Ibid.*, p. 366. Thus the Möbius strip, by its always doubling inscription, formalizes what Freud defined as overdetermination.

But this interpretation would be an error, because time (hence historical differentiation and the possibility of the inscription of an epistemological rupture on the strip) is essential to the constitution of the Möbius strip. The circling itself introduces the necessity of time in the strip. We have a return, but one of difference, not of the same—which accounts, for example, for the expansion of modern science as depending on time and the possibility of conceptualizing an epistemological rupture. Lacan tries to conceptualize science, contrary to Nietzsche, in whose work the idea of science is represented only on the side of the scientist's unconscious desire.

In other words, between the mythological repetition of the Nietzschean return of the same, and the logical reinscription of an object on both the side of exactitude and the side of truth, there is an insurmountable gap.

The Möbius strip accounts for three different operations: (1) it is a description of the subject of science (our homunculus), taking into account its internal/external division and sleepwalking between truth and exactitude, while being submitted to the expansion without limit of mathematization; (2) it is a figuration of the paradoxical relationship between knowledge and conjecture; and finally (3) it is a metaphor of Lacan's epistemological intervention itself, as he makes exactitude and meaning the respective correlatives of one another (it should be noted that the epistemological cut here has the paradoxical figure of a cohesion).

We have to stress at this point that the tridimensional Möbius strip defines a void in its center (absent from the two-dimensional strip in Fig. 2–9 with which we began our little exercise in topology), whose function is all-important: the hole represents with the same stroke the incompleteness of science and the resistance of the unconscious to formalization. This void is not the empty set $\{\phi\}$ of mathematics: it is filled by the objects that escape formalization either by science or psychoanalysis. It should be clear to the reader, at this point, that Lacan's goal is no other than to produce the overlapping of the hole of knowledge and the hole of meaning.

The resistance to or repression of formalization of the unconscious by the ego points to a rich paradox in Lacan's theory. On one hand, as we have seen, the subject of psychoanalysis cannot be differentiated from the subject of science. Stated in another way, psychoanalysis is inherently modern; if not, it is only an art of interpretation that repeats magical, mythological, or religious processes. On the other hand, science is the abolition of the subject.[59] This is easy to demonstrate, again, by the example of life insurance; we do not enter the insurance companies' calculation as singular subjects, life insurance has no interests in our particulars. We figure in the calculation of risk as yet another factor. Similarly, Einstein's (or Freud's inasmuch as it belongs to modern science) theories have nothing to do with the personalities of Einstein or Freud, or with them as subjects.

Regarding the abolition of the subject, we can detect in Lacan a certain fatalism: the expansion of science that produces it is not stoppable, we cannot turn our back on the procedures and logic of modern science; in particular, theoretical psychoanalysis cannot avoid the determinism found in the real (logical) structure of the signifier. By the same token, we can find no recourse against the abolition of the subject by science through the traditional means of consolation or protection, as in the reinforcing of the ego (which is for Lacan but a reinforcing of an illusion), Eastern mysticism, or magical thought (which makes us pretend that we are the source of the structure and that we can modify it at will). Any recourse to the traditional refuges of irrationality would be in vain; they are but a return of the repressed that has no way of ensuring that we have a handle on our abolition by science. Briefly, rationality cannot be countered by irrationality (and sometimes, alas, vice versa).

Psychoanalysis allows us to recognize clearly this paradox and this impasse, and Lacan offers, in the seminar on ethics (*Séminaire VIII*) a psychoanalytical solution. He repeats that the cure should prompt us not to make any concessions about our desire. This is in itself a paradoxical imperative, since we are not able to completely penetrate the figures of our desire because they are unconscious. But, in light of the abolition of the subject by science, the prescription makes sense (and it probably makes sense only in this framework): the desire of the subject is the last line of resistance to its abolition by science, the affirmation of what is irreducible to an algorithm: the restoration of the subject in its symbolic and unconscious dimension.

---

59. See for example *Autres écrits*, p. 151.

Freud saw four main factors that constituted the resistance to psychoanalysis. He attributed the resistance to the newness of his ideas, prudery in regard to the sexual content of his theories, anti-Semitism of the society at large and within the psychiatric community, and finally resistance to science itself. Lacan offers us a different and more general take. Freud, here more optimistic than usual, supposes in humankind a *Wissentrieb*, an unconscious drive to know. Hence the desire for the progress of knowledge would be firmly entrenched in the human psyche and in the end, supposedly, rationality would prevail. For Lacan, there is no such thing as a *Wissentrieb*; the unconscious already knows everything that it needs to know (oedipal configuration, absence of sexual rapport, etc.) and doesn't desire to know more.[60] Hence, the demand for knowledge comes from the superego or the ego, and is a sublimation or a repression of a sexual drive.

Lacan deduces that humanity as such doesn't desire to know. Especially, it doesn't want to know about science or the unconscious, men in this regard having a passion for ignorance. Men don't want to know about science, because they intuitively feel it leads to the abolition of the subject; they don't want to know about the unconscious, because it shatters the illusion of an autonomous and free-willing ego. Since the analyst alone among men desires to know, he is truly "a litter of humanity."[61]

The human passion for ignorance is a passion for happiness, or in other words an attempt at preserving the narcissistic illusions of the ego. Therefore, humanity loathes knowledge that runs contrary to this aim, and the psychoanalyst can only inspire horror in the common man; Lacan went so far as to say that the psychoanalyst was himself often horrified by his own act.

We now need to go further, and to ask, What is the status of psychoanalysis amid the conflict of disciplines and fields? Lacan seems to be of two minds on the subject, oscillating between science and non-science. But in fact his take is (as usual) coherent. On one hand, "the praxis of psychoanalysis is applied only to the subject of science,"[62] a

---

60. *Séminaire XVII*, p. 33.

61. See "Note italienne," *Autres écrits*, p. 308. See also the analyst as a saint, as developed by "Télévision," *Autres écrits*, p. 520.

62. *Écrits*, p. 863.

principle that may shock humanists. On the other hand, there is a limit to the expansion of logic and mathematical formalizations: "Through logic, the psychoanalytic discourse touches the real, when it encounters it as impossible. Hence it is this discourse that carries logic to its ultimate power as a science of the real."[63]

In other words, scientific rigor (which, despite the rumor, Lacan strictly adheres to and follows) finds its limit with what it cannot analyze, the singularity presented by the analysand's case. Lacan says that psychoanalysis as a practice is a "trick" that presupposes know-how but not necessarily theorization: "The analytical trick will not be mathematical. That is why analytical discourse differs from scientific discourse."[64] The cure, with its singularities, cannot be made to fit into a conceptual box. Hence, Lacan said that it was not necessary to be a Lacanian to be a good analyst.

Psychoanalysis is therefore split in two: it uses the scientific process as a theory, and the learning curve of corporations (in the medieval sense of the term) as a practice. It is good, for a psychoanalyst, to know and understand Lacan. But it is neither necessary nor sufficient: the psychoanalyst has to learn know-how by undergoing a psychoanalysis him- or herself.

If we go back to Galileo, we notice in his work two kinds of experiments: crucial ones and mental ones (*experimentum crucis* and *experimentum mentis*);[65] the mental experiment is defined by the calculation of the effects another calculation can have. The crucial experiment happens when the calculation is realized in nature. We can argue with Imre Lakatos[66] that, in modern science, there are no crucial experiments, only mental ones, because a statement on nature can be contradicted only by another statement, not by an experiment. Experiments in science are the results of a prior calculation; when this calculation fails, we need to modify it and recalculate the experiment itself. *Sensu stricto*, Lacan does not make a distinction between *experiment* in science

63. "L'Étourdit," *Autres écrits*, p. 449.

64. *Séminaire XX*, p. 105.

65. Galileo Galilei, *Dialogue Concerning the Two Chief World Systems*; Berkeley: Univ. of Cal. Press, 1962, p. 145. See François Regnault, *Lacan and Experience, op. cit.*

66. See Chapter 10 of Lakatos's *Mathematics, Science and Epistemology, Philosophical Papers*, vol. 2; Cambridge, UK: Cambridge University Press, 1978.

and *experiment* in theoretical psychoanalysis: "The experience of the unconscious at the level where I put it is not distinguishable from an experiment in physics. It is also external to the subject."[67]

If we now apply the distinction between *experimentum mentis* and *experimentum crucis* to psychoanalysis, we may call the analysis itself of and by a patient a *crucial* experiment, whereas the reflection on this experiment, its analogy with other cases, and the theoretical developments it leads to constitute a *mental* experiment. Hence, if there are no crucial experiments in science, there are in psychoanalysis, and these are called cases. The collection of all the cases constitutes the *experimenta mentis* of psychoanalysis.

Applied psychoanalysis (the cure of singular cases) therefore cannot be entirely formalized according to scientific procedures. In that sense, there is no "science of the cure." Moreover, an analysand's crucial experiment is always a singularity. Hence, a case functions at the same time as an illustration for clinical categories, but also as an exception to them through its singularity. François Regnault has elegantly summarized this apparent paradox: "A case is an exception to the law it belongs to."[68]

Lacan concedes the point to Karl Popper, who denied psychoanalysis a scientific character, but only insofar as the cure is concerned. Popper (1983) argues that psychoanalysis is not a science because its results cannot be contradicted (*falsified*, in his vocabulary). Without Popper being aware of it, this is indeed a rephrasing of Freud, telling us that the unconscious doesn't know contradiction. Lacan adds precision to this nonfalsifiable nature of the unconscious. For him, at the center of psychoanalysis lies the paradigm positing that the sexual rapport is not writable in a logical form, that it is impossible to write it: "If you don't test the sexual rapport through writing, [. . .] you cannot reach the goal that I proposed to psychoanalysis, to be equal to a science. In order to reach this goal, you have to demonstrate that the sexual rapport cannot possibly be written. In this, it is not affirmable nor refutable: it is like truth."[69]

---

67. *Autres écrits*, p. 148. This is congruent with the external materiality of the Symbolic–Real axis.

68. See François Regnault, "Lacan and Experience," *op cit.*, p. 47.

69. *Autres écrits*, p. 310.

Hence, the inexistence of the sexual rapport makes it irrefutably nonaffirmable according to the logical procedures of science, which need an expressed proposition in order to falsify it: "As Karl Popper abundantly showed, psychoanalysis is not at all a science, because it is irrefutable. It is a practice, a practice that will last as long it will last. It is a chatting practice."[70] The heart of psychoanalysis is not subjected to science. This is owing to the nature of the unconscious, which, according to Freud's description, doesn't know contradiction: "It is said that the unconscious doesn't know contradiction. That is why the analyst has to operate through something which is not grounded on contradiction,"[71] that is, through a discourse that is not scientific. However, the mental experiment that theoretical psychoanalysis represents is. In particular, it can and has to be falsified, each time, through a crucial experiment represented by the singularity of each case.

Modern science, as abolition or erasure of the subject of the unconscious, is absolute and extreme repression; its expansion in the contemporary world lets us foresee more and more uncontrollable returns of the repressed (in issues of identity or ethnic politics and wars), which will struggle against science's superegotistical imposition.

As far as Lacan is concerned, his formalized theory is itself a form of the repression of the unconscious subject, hence it has to be corrected. Lacan struggled against this abolition of the subject in many ways: by the way he spoke, interpreted, wrote, and taught, by his wordplay and jokes, and by all those interventions that evoked his singularity and introduced breathing space in his relentless drive to submit his discourse to modern logic and mathematics. But he also put a brake on the expansion of modern science in his own discourse at a more general level by proposing an ethics for psychoanalysis.

---

70. *Omicar?* no. 19, 1979, p. 5. See Lacan's "Discourse de clôture du congrès de l'École freudienne sur la transmission," in *Lettres de l'École freudienne*, no. 25, 1979: "The unconscious explains everything, but, as Karl Popper put it, it explains too much. The unconscious is a conjecture that cannot be refuted." See also Karl Popper's criticism of the scientific basis of psychoanalysis in *Realism and the Aim of Science*; Totowa, NJ: Rowman and Littlefield, 1983, pp. 40–44.

71. *Ibid.*, p. 8.

AN IMPOSSIBLE ETHICS

The problem is this: How can one preserve the singularity of a subject, his desire, his case, when the expansion of science in Lacan himself erases this singularity either in clinical categories (psychosis, neurosis, hysteria) or in mathematical formalization?

Freud had already remarked on the difficulties that confronted subjects in a modern context. In fact, in his pessimistic view, modernity, under the guise of the expansion of modern science, is always a reinforcement of the superego (see, for example, *Civilization and Its Discontents*, published in 1930). As Lacan states: "In Freud's theoretical developments, the origin of the moral dimension is rooted nowhere else than in desire itself."[72] This development imposes harder and harder tasks on man; progress, for Freud, can be summarized as a more and more efficacious repression, which lets one foresee wilder and more uncontrollable returns of the repressed, Nazism's rise being here the crucial example.

In the *Séminaire VIII, L'ethique de la psychanalyse*, Lacan builds his answer to the expansion of science, which is synonymous with the abolition of the subject of desire. This answer can be summarized as an ethics of singularity.

As such, it upsets the entire philosophical tradition on the problem of ethics; whether in Aristotle (*The Nichomachean Ethics*) or Kant, ethics are always concerned with a human community: it is an ethics of the common good. The individual good is always subordinated to the good of groups, whatever their historical definitions are. And if we follow Lacan on this path, we can even argue that the politics of sexual identities (lesbian, gay, etc.), inasmuch as they are not concerned by singularities, are at the service of repression: by agglomerating singular subjects, they suppress them.

In broader terms, Lacan's ethics is not an ethics of the law, that is, not a moral system intended to attenuate guilt. Law and desire, as we have seen, are dialectically bound; the existence of each depends on the other. Any desire will immediately create its opposite, repression, and the ensuing guilt: for psychoanalysis, "the Sovereign Good,

---

72. *Séminaire VII, Le transfert*, p. 11.

who is the mother as the object of incest, is a forbidden good, and there is no other good."[73]

This is how Lacan rewrites and justifies psychoanalytically the Biblical motive of originary guilt. Therefore, Lacanian ethics are not a hedonism, such as the pursuit of pleasure recommended, for example, by the Epicureans in the philosophical tradition of antiquity. In more contemporary terms, Lacan stresses the complete failure of all the experiences of sexual liberation, which have missed the renewal of guilt inevitably associated with the emphasis on pleasure.

As far as subjects are concerned, Lacan proposes an ethics of singularity: "This truth that we are seeking in a concrete experience is not the truth of a superior law. If the truth we are seeking is a liberating truth, it is a truth that we seek where our subject hides it. It is a singular truth."[74]

It is an ethics of resistance to the superegotistical expansion of science, in which the only sin is to make concessions about one's desire,[75] and the only responsibility is to take upon oneself one's position as a subject.

On the psychoanalyst's side, this ethics of singularity intervenes in the transference, and Lacan reduces it to the analyst's duty of a proper intervention that will underline the crucial moments in the analysand's discourse. He summarized the psychoanalyst's duty in his answer to Jacques-Alain Miller's question in *Télévision*:

"*What should I do?* The answer is simple. That is what I do: I extract from my practice the ethics of speaking well."[76]

This call for an ethics of singularity (of desire) is at the same time entirely logical (it is the only form the subject can oppose to its own abolition by science) and paradoxical: How can we not make concessions about our desire, if, according to Lacan, it is unconscious, and therefore impossible to incarnate in an image? How can we resist the expansion of the superego if it is also beyond the reach of our consciousness?

---

73. *Séminaire VII*, p. 85.
74. *Séminaire VII*, p. 32.
75. *Séminaire VII*, p. 370.
76. "Télévision," *Autres écrits*, p. 541.

The answer, for the psychoanalyst, is to take subjects one by one, and always stress the ability of singular analysands to tolerate finally what is a structural lack of figuration for the unconscious core of our being. As far as the broader society is concerned, Lacanian ethics may be summarized as a word of caution about the repression of singular desires, lest they reappear under the wildest, most aggressive forms of the return of what was repressed.

3

The Master, the Academic, the Psychoanalyst, and the Hysteric: Four Discourses

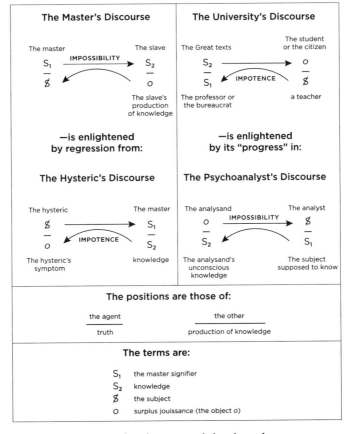

Figure 3–1. The diagram of the four discourses.

Lacan proposed a theory of discourses in the *Séminaire XVII*, which took place from 1969 to 1970; he distinguishes four of them: the Master's, the University's, the psychoanalyst's, and the hysteric's, while not ruling out the existence of other discourses;[1] these were, however, the dominant ones against which he wanted to position the specificity of psychoanalysis.

What is a discourse? It is a formalizable structure that positions itself in between language and speech. It can subsist without being spoken by an individual (as in the case of an institution), but it is not the whole of a language: it inscribes itself in language as a fundamental relationship. Located in between the generality of a given language and the speech act of an individual or the extreme singularity of each human subject, discourses define social groups. They represent the specific structure in which individuals belonging to this group will inscribe themselves (even without them knowing it); they formalize their symbolic and social belonging. A discourse operates the relationship of one signifier to another signifier: "The discourses in question are the signifying articulation, the apparatus, whose sole presence and existing status dominates and governs everything that can emerge as speech. There are discourses without speech, which comes afterward to inhabit them."[2] Consistent with his aspiration to make a minimal complete transmission of theoretical psychoanalysis, Lacan confesses that he would like to erase the presence of the Master teacher by ceding it to a "discourse without speech,"[3] an algorithm functioning without his person. His speech, by his own admission, is encumbered with projections and identifications and thus an obstacle to the purer transmission of his formalized discourse.[4]

In Lacan's formalization, the general model is a quaternary group, a matrix. Each discourse is defined by four positions supporting four terms. Starting with the Master's discourse, by keeping the positions but revolving the terms a quarter turn counterclockwise, we can generate the three other discourses. The four discourses, in their turn, will form another quaternary matrix.

---

1. By reordering the terms' succession, it is possible to generate sixteen discourses.

2. *Séminaire XVII*, p. 194.

3. "When will you see that I prefer a discourse without speech?" *Autres écrits*, p. 371.

4. *Autres écrits*, p. 304.

Let us first examine the four positions. The *agent*, as the name indicates, is the one who acts. The *other* is the one who is acted upon, as the vector indicates. The *Master* acts on the slave, the *Professor* on the student, the *Analysand* on the analyst, the *Hysteric* on the father. As always in Lacan, statements are always addressed to somebody: the quadripodes show a structure common to at least two subjects who have internalized the matrix. This (speech) act—a command, a symbolic pact that is the actualization of a discourse—forces the other to a production of knowledge (the production of goods being dependent on a know-how, an ordering of signifiers, before it is realized in the material world). On the left-hand side, you will have an individual or an institution, and on the right the individuals or groups who are acted upon. The "quadripode" formalizes their social interaction.

This interaction is noted by vectors, which, in certain discourses, are qualified by impossibility or impotence. Impossibility signifies the encounter with something real that is not reducible; for example, and to anticipate, the master's will and desire cannot be totally satisfied by the slave: the master cannot exhaust his desire by consuming the slave's production. To suppose otherwise would be akin to admitting that the master's desire can be entirely fulfilled, and thus would also be entirely conscious, a logical impossibility in a universe that acknowledges the existence of the unconscious.

Impotence is different; it consists in the fact that production has no relation to truth, hence it masks a real impossibility; as an example, Lacan mentions the impotence of the University's discourse at producing a thinking subject.[5]

Finally, each discourse's quadripode is positioned as to form a quaternary matrix, thereby defining the structure that presides over the interactions between the respective discourses (more on this later).

Definitions of Terms

Now, the terms; the master-signifier is, very briefly, a subject defined by a proper name:[6] what links a person to his or her singular and unconscious being. S_2 is the set of signifiers, or, in a restricted sense, a

5. *Séminaire XVII*, p. 203.
6. See Chapter 2 of this volume, p. 48.

corpus of knowledge (the slave's knowledge, in the case of the Master's discourse, the canon of great books or authors in the University's discourse, the writings or edicts of the "fathers of the revolution"). If a subject S_1 positions itself relative to a knowledge S_2, then a barred subject $\mathcal{S}$ will be created; to speak, for Lacan, is to produce a subject divided between its conscious knowledge and its unconscious desire. Finally, o is the now familiar o object that causes desire. But in his late elaboration, Lacan specifies it as surplus jouissance (use, enjoyment, orgasm), a concept he modeled according to Marx's elaboration of surplus value. If jouissance is the process where, at the very moment desire reaches its object, it loses it, then jouissance can be grasped only through what is left of it—a surplus, a leftover, a failure, a loss—and surplus jouissance is the leftover of the erasure of jouissance, when satisfied.

Let us go through each of the discourses to make the matrix clearer.

THE MASTER'S DISCOURSE

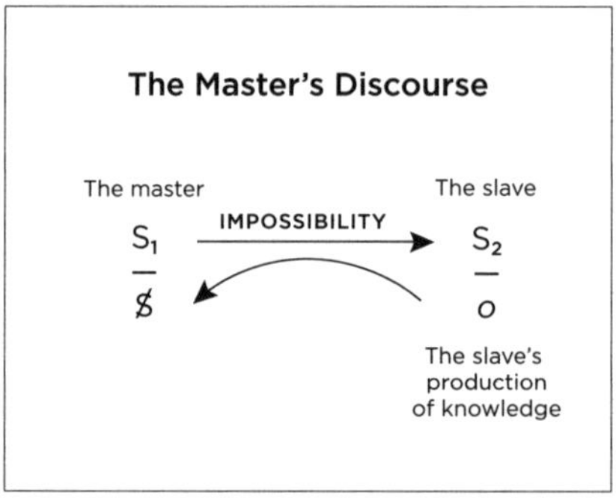

Figure 3–2.

We can position on the left-hand side the Master, on the right the slave. S_1 will be the signifier that defines the Master's essence. S_2 will be the slave's knowledge. This knowledge produces objects (of desire –o) that are appropriated by the Master. Hence the slave doesn't have access to them: he produces so that the Master can destroy (consume) his production.[7]

---

7. A good example is seen in the way Socrates (S_1), in the Platonic dialogue *Meno* (ed. G. M. Grube; Indianapolis: Hackett, 1980), always tries to extract from

But this consuming of objects or knowledge cannot satiate the Master's desire; indeed, it makes manifest that he is barred from this unconscious desire's satisfaction, which is the Master's truth; while he enjoys (or consumes and destroys) the fruits of the slave's labor, the Master is barred from his own truth as a subject ($).

The (illusory) presupposition of this discourse is that something can be organized in a totality (S_2): the slaves, a nation, an ethnic group, or an electorate, on which the Master will act: "The idea that knowledge can become a totality is immanent to politics as such."[8] In other words, the Master's discourse is prey to the omnipotence of thought (as developed by Freud in *Totem and Taboo*, first published in 1912), which is convinced that to think is to do; thinking is then the totality of reality. The Master's discourse thus forecloses the truth that all knowledge is by structure and definition incomplete.

We can also infer that, through its aspiration to totality, the Master's discourse formalizes even its contradiction: Revolution. Inasmuch as the revolted slave simply aspires to the Master's position (thereby aspiring to be the master of people who will be *his* slaves), he doesn't affect the basic structure of the Master's discourse, which "encompasses everything, even what believes itself to be a revolution."[9] Revolution, in conformity to its etymology, is truly just a repositioning of opposites, leaving the structure of the Master's discourse unaffected.

For Lacan, there is a deep affinity between the discourse of philosophy and the Master's discourse; they show the same attempt at totalization, of which Hegel is a preeminent paradigm: "Hegel's discourse is a master's discourse, which is grounded on the substitution of the master by the State through the long way of culture, to reach absolute knowledge."[10]

The Master's discourse is, then, the formalization of politics itself, to which philosophy serves as a help by giving it the "reason" to justify

<hr>

manual (i.e., slavish) labor (S_2) the metaphors that in fact describe the philosopher's activity: "Philosophy in its historical function is the extraction, the betrayal I daresay, of the slave's knowledge, in order to obtain from it its transmutation in the Master's knowledge." *Séminaire XVII*, p. 22.

8. *Séminaire XVII*, p. 33.

9. *Ibid.*, p. 99.

10. *Séminaire XVII*, p. 90.

totalization: "Metaphysics is only (and can last only as) what plugs the hole of politics."[11]

Hegel, and the dialectics of the master and the slave, are the first reference to politics in modern times for Lacan. Hegel is read through two main criticisms; first, the dialectics of the master and the slave forget to include language in the process; yet both the master and the slave have their position determined by a more powerful master than either of them can imagine. Indeed, it is impossible to usurp the master's position without having it designated in advance by a name. The master is always a usurper precisely because he feigns that he is able to derive his position from himself, erasing the fact that he occupies it only because the designation allows him to do so. The source of his power is a signifying, linguistic structure, which he conveniently forgets. In other words, the dialectics erase the unconscious.

Indeed the master–slave dialectic (the true engine of all human history according to Hegel) presupposes that it plays itself out in the realm of a (self revelatory) consciousness totally conscious of itself: the Hegelian notion of an absolute knowledge depends on that. In other words, the possibility of a hidden, unconscious knowledge simply doesn't exist for Hegel, and, as in all logic, the subject must know himself entirely to access absolute knowledge.

Second, Lacan denies the Hegelian (and then Marxian) possibility that the production of material goods by the slave (or the proletarian) may ever produce symbolic values and be the basis of a new, revolutionary organization of society. Why is that so? Because, by skipping the primary step of language as what organizes production and its corresponding social positioning, Hegel is bound to fancy that praxis can secrete symbolic values. In reality, there is no such secretion, and Lacan defies anybody to bring forth proof that, from work, something like a concept could emanate. Production and social hierarchies have always already been determined by a signifying chain: to alter them means to alter the structure itself, an endeavor, as we have already ascertained,[12]

---

11. "Introduction à l'édition allemande des Écrits," *Scilicet* 5, 1975, p. 13. The example chosen to illustrate the temptation of totality is here "my 'friend' Heidegger"; for Lacan, Heidegger's espousal of Nazi politics was not an accident or a deviation, but was inherent to his own philosophy.

12. See above.

notoriously hard, if not impossible, to achieve. The actors of history may switch places, but has the deep structure that positions them changed? That is the question, and the answer is most often negative because of the existence of the unconscious. The locus of this deep structure is beyond will and consciousness.[13]

If Marx is not disentangled from the Hegelian error of considering labor (and not language) as a source of concepts, however, Lacan does credit him with being "the inventor of the symptom": "Marxism opens up the question that discourse is tied to the subject's interests."[14] Marx's theory in some way anticipates psychoanalysis; it has some relationship with it because it also takes the existence of the unconscious into account—as Hegel does not.

The symptom, as Marx formulates it in his theory, is for Lacan none other than *Mehrwert*, the surplus value that he discovers as the fundamental notion of capitalistic economy. It is basically the value the laborer creates without being paid for, and which the capitalist despoils him of. For Lacan, this value has two fundamental characteristics: it can be subjected to a mathematical operation (as Marx did), but it cannot be represented by a quantity or a number—that is why classical economists don't accept Marx's concept of surplus value. In other words, it is the repressed (unconscious) symptom of capitalistic exploitation that evokes, not a quantity, but a symbolic value. Capitalism produces not only goods, but first and foremost concepts, as does any human activity. Goods are submitted to a discursive structure. A car, for example, is the result of calculations, design, and know-how aimed at satisfying consumers' requests. Production is then only interpretable in terms of signifiers: in Lacan, *Mehrwert* becomes *Mehrlust*, or *Marxlust*, the surplus jouissance.[15] In other words, the spoliation of the worker by the master (capital) is not a monetary one, but a spoliation of knowledge, of symbolic jouissance; to reduce the worker to a mere quantitative value is also a symbolic operation. "Marx denounces the worker's spoliation of surplus value. But he does it without realizing that the spo-

---

13. See, among others, the developments in "Subversion of the Subject and Dialectics of Desire," in *Écrits, a Selection* (English), pp. 296–297.

14. *Séminaire XVII*, p. 105.

15. *Séminaire XVII*, p. 56.

liation's secret is in knowledge itself—as is the secret of the laborer being reduced to a pure value."[16]

The Master's discourse becomes then the discourse of capitalism in the nineteenth century, where the owners of the capital dispossess the laborers of their production and in turn spoliate themselves of surplus jouissance in order to reinvest in the production machine. In modern times, the laborers are replaced by the consumers themselves, who are a product of the consumer society.[17] The proletarian has become the consumer—that is, he has become interested in the survival of production. This evolution of pure capitalism is the condition of its own survival. In other words, present-day capitalism redistributes the surplus jouissance to the workers in order that it may continue to endure.

The knowledge produced by capitalism is an alienation of desire by the request for goods. For example, a consumer society like ours aims at satisfying yearnings by offering substitutes, the objects of industrial production, that are even more removed from the real object of desire than sexualized ones: "In the master's discourse it is surplus jouissance which satisfies the subject only because it only sustains the reality of fantasy."[18] The surplus jouissance of capitalism is therefore the acme of alienation. Again, we should view Lacan's take on capitalism as an analysis that doesn't necessarily lead to a moral condemnation. After all, our mode of being in reality is alienation itself.

Hence, Lacan puts himself in the position of redrawing the analysis of capitalistic production from the point of view of the unconscious (the Analyst's discourse): it is "the extensive, hence insatiable, production of a lack of jouissance"[19]—that is, the infinite production of objects of desire that infinitely deepen the alienation of desire: "The lack of jouissance is in a process of accumulation on one side (this is what we commonly call 'savings') to accumulate the means of this production as capital. On the other side, it extends consumption, without which this production would be in vain, precisely because it is incapable of procuring a jouissance that would slow it (the production)."[20]

---

16. *Séminaire XVII*, p. 92.
17. *Ibid.*, p. 35.
18. "L'Étourdit," *Autres écrits*, p. 445.
19. "Radiophonie," *Autres écrits*, p. 435.
20. *Ibid.*

As far as politics goes, in a modern democracy, the Master is paradoxically everybody's and anybody's slave: he has to be elected by a vote, hence he has to seek the majority's approval; only then he is recognized as "the Master."

We can also use the Lacanian discourses to classify some varieties of mental disturbance. The kernel of this development is to be found in Freud's *Totem and Taboo*, where Freud writes, "We may say that hysteria is a caricature of an artistic creation, a compulsion neurosis, a caricature of a religion, and a paranoiac delusion, a caricature of a philosophical system."[21] The Master's discourse then takes the form of a mental illness: psychosis. As the master reduces his world to mere consciousness (barring his access to the unconscious), so the psychotic operates the "foreclusion" (*Verwerfung* in Freud's lexicon) of the Name-of-the Father,[22] and thus constitutes his discourse as the totality of the world he lives in. Psychosis presupposes a totality, an illusion that reinforces its delusional mastery. This totality, Lacan emphasizes, is fully coherent, and this coherence in itself is the sign of the psychotic's delirium (as well as the dictator's and the philosopher's): in other words, the master doesn't tolerate rebellion, the dictator opposition, the philosopher contradiction, whereas the structure in fact creates its own antithesis. The only true opposition to the Master's discourse comes from the Analyst's, which is then (like the Hysteric's) defined as a discourse of nonmastery, and hence, in the general matrix, is positioned exactly opposite to the Master's.[23] Why is that so? Because, contrary to the Master's and the University's, the discourses of the analyst and the hysteric both deal with the unconscious, which is not masterable; in other words, they don't presuppose a totality, but face an incompleteness. This failure of completeness is either repressed or foreclosed in the first two discourses; in their own way, they don't want to know anything about it.

The rebellious students of May 68 were very surprised to learn from Lacan's mouth that they were seeking a Master—so surprised, in fact,

---

21. Freud, *Totem and Taboo*, Chapter II, section 4.

22. "The foreclusion of the Name-of-the-Father in lieu of the Other, and the failure of the paternal metaphor gives to psychosis its essential condition, as well as the structure that differentiates psychosis from neurosis." *Écrits*, p. 575.

23. "The master's discourse is the reverse of the analyst's." "Radiophonie," *Autres écrits*, p. 88.

that they didn't understand a word. Invited to speak at the University of Vincennes, he said:

> "If you were a little patient, and if you wished for our impromptus to go on, I would tell you that the revolutionary yearning will always end up in the master's discourse. Experience proves it.
> "What you yearn for as revolutionaries is a master. You will have it."
> *Intervention*—"We have one, we have Pompidou."
> "You fancy that you have a master in Pompidou. What the heck is this all about?"[24]

This take on the students' revolution proceeds first from earlier developments of Hegel's concept of the "beautiful soul." In Lacan's reading, the romantic beautiful soul projects onto the outside world the disorders that affect it as a subject, thereby inverting the causality of disturbance and absolving itself of its responsibility as subject.[25] But the analysis is also derived from the four discourses, formalized in that year's seminar, which Lacan put on the blackboard for his intervention at the University of Vincennes. Revolution, in trying to make a pseudo-totality out of a group (the bourgeoisie, the proletariat, etc.), will ineluctably inscribe itself either in the Master's or the University's discourse: the students of May 68 in Paris were indeed, through their acts and speeches, looking for a master without knowing it. Their subversion was in fact a reconfirmation of the unconscious structure silently at work in the Master's discourse.

This may look like a conservative (and desperate) view of history, where the deep structure of discourse remains forever unaffected, although allowing the switching of positions (e.g., the slave comes to occupy the locus of the master). Lacan cites communism as an example: "Communists, when they form in the bourgeois order a counter-society, only mimic all the themes of this order: work, family, and country are the leitmotivs they oppose to anybody who would void their own paradoxes."[26]

However, Lacan proposes an alternative to this eternal turn of the wheels of fortune and politics, which is none other than the Analyst's discourse: "The psychoanalytical discourse is precisely the one that can ground a social link cleansed of any grouping constraint."[27]

---

24. *Séminaire XVII*, p. 239.
25. *Écrits*, p. 173.
26. "Radiophonie," *Autres écrits*, p. 440.
27. "L'Étourdit," *Autres écrits*, p. 474.

In other words, the Analyst's discourse is the only one that takes into account the individual's unconscious singularity (desire). The other discourses either foreclose it (the Master's), repress it (the University's), or abolish it (science's). This focus on the unconscious is precisely what allows the rereading and critique of the other discourses. Hence, psychoanalysis, with its "raking light," the peculiar enlightenment it provides, will allow you better to situate yourself as a singularity with respect to all the discourses that want to ascribe you to a group—of voters, of consumers, of ethnic, sexual, racial belonging, and so on.

How can Lacan conceive of the Analyst's discourse, focused on a singularity, as a social discourse? Because it cannot be conducted by oneself, the analysand needing another person to really analyze what is in his or her unconscious. In that sense, Freud never analyzed himself: self-analysis is an oxymoron.

Thus, in taking subjects one by one, psychoanalysis forbids their dissolution in imaginary groupings, those which the master or the academic always presuppose as a condition of their discursive operation.

THE UNIVERSITY'S DISCOURSE

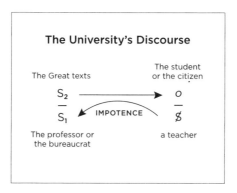

Figure 3–3.

Let's move another quarter-turn counterclockwise. What is now in the dominant position of the agent? Not a person under the guise of its master signifier, as in the Master's discourse, but S_2, that is, a corpus of knowledge, and more precisely, a collection of "sacred" texts. On the left, the canon, the great texts (as read or applied under the bar by the theologian, the professor, or the bureaucrat), on the right, the student or the citizen of a bureaucracy.

If we look at the constitution of the University's discourse as born from the colleges of theology in the Middle Ages, these sacred texts were the Bible, but also what the church considered to be the *auctoritates*: those Bible commentaries by the church's fathers that were deemed to be authoritative. Later, during the Renaissance, when the humanists began to give classical authors the same weight the Biblical tradition had enjoyed, the same authority was conferred on the culture of antiquity. Then, during the Romantic period, it was the turn of contemporary authors' books (a stage we have not overcome yet) to occupy the position of the agent.

Lacan defines the functioning of this know-it-all knowledge as essentially bureaucratic.[28] It knows, but not the truth, even if it takes itself for the totality of reality. The object of the process is not the truth, but the application of texts to the student or the citizen who is located on the right-hand side of the algorithm. As such, the University's discourse includes not only theology and scholasticism, not only classical authors or the canon of modern masters, but also Marx, Stalin, Lenin, and the edicts of our legislative bodies. "The Great Man has said this, so we apply it, and you, the student or the citizen, perform it no matter what": such would be the basic statement of the University's discourse; it is fundamentally a quotation discourse. In that sense, the huge bureaucratic weight of our institutions, especially evident in our universities, owes nothing to chance.

The professor or the bureaucrat is (S_1) under the S_2 of knowledge: his or her functions are reduced to being the keeper and transmitter of the canonical texts, and to forcing their application on the student or the citizen. The bar that separates them from the canon indicates their noninvolvement. What is produced by this functioning is not a truth, but a divided subject, one who is impotent in the attempt to become a master-signifier; the keepers of the canon or the bureaucrats are not allowed to question the truth of the texts.

The goal of the operation is none other than to allow the self-reproduction of the university's discourse, by producing (from the student or the citizen) yet another teacher or bureaucrat who will faithfully

---

28. *Ibid.*, p. 34.

apply the great texts to future students or aspiring citizens. Like the Master's discourse (which wishes to eternalize the slave's production and its consumption by the master), the University's discourse insures its self-reproduction by fabricating the future keepers of the great texts—teachers or bureaucrats.

The University's discourse can also affect psychoanalysis, when this field wants to integrate itself into academia. Psychoanalysis will then borrow the quotational mode of the university: "Freud said . . . Lacan said," with no regard for the conceptual structure from which Lacan's or Freud's constructions derive their truth.

It is easy to demonstrate the usefulness of Lacan's formalization with a specific example, as the contemporary University's discourse has been submitted to a mutation in the humanities. Here, by fabricating apologists for victimology, it has become increasingly politicized. In fact, this can be seen as the symptom of a regression to the Master's discourse, where the goal is no longer the study of the great texts, but the production of victims who have no other hope than to aspire (by a revolution of words) to the Master's position. Given the close relationship between the two discourses, maybe this was unavoidable. As Lacan said, not without his trademark humor: "The university's discourse is the master's discourse, but reinforced with obscurantism."[29] Or, elsewhere: "The university discourse conveys the master's, but only by liberating the latter from truth."[30] This transference from one form to another is understandable only in psychoanalytical terms.

The University's discourse doesn't want to know a thing about the real, the unconscious:[31] it is an essential nominalism, where names don't evoke a truth,[32] but are the authoritative references to conform to.

It thus also defines a form of mental perturbation: compulsion neurosis, as it represses the truth. The University discourse's mechanism

---

29. "Radiophonie," *Autres écrits*, p. 88.

30. "Préface à une thèse," *Autres écrits*; p. 396.

31. This explains psychoanalysis's minimal penetration in universities around the world: it is a matter of structure. Freud wished that medical students (especially psychiatrists and psychologists) would be acquainted with psychoanalysis, but he thought that an academic formation was not necessary to the psychoanalyst (see *Standard Edition*, vol. 18, pp. 170–173).

32. "Préface à une thèse," *ibid.*

is then the Freudian *Verdrängung*, repression. The neurotic installs himself in the locus of the Other (the canon, the great texts) and plays dead: he substracts himself from the risks of truth and death.[33]

THE PSYCHOANALYST'S DISCOURSE

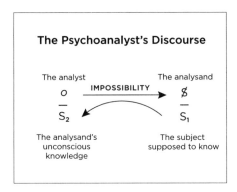

Figure 3–4.

On the left is the psychoanalyst, on the right, the analysand or patient. This is the only discourse that takes into account the unconscious. As such, it is the exact opposite of the Master's discourse, because it posits in its center a thing that is not masterable (the Master's discourse has foreclosed its access to the unconscious by forcing everything to depend on consciousness). Indeed, the Psychoanalyst's discourse is the only one that doesn't take itself for truth: it knows that truth is external to discourse (that is, unconscious), whereas the master and the university present their construction as truth itself: "The psychoanalytic discourse is the only one that doesn't take itself for truth."[34] This means that the Analyst's discourse is the only one to posit that truth is outside of any discourse, because it is unconscious. This recognition allows the analyst's discourse to project an oblique light on the other discourses that work under the illusion they can master truth.

---

33. *Écrits*, p. 811 (English, p. 309).
34. "Peut-être à Vincennes," *Ornicar?* 1, 1975.

The means of operation of the Analyst's discourse is an artificial hysterization that applies to men and women alike: as soon as the analysand enters analysis, he or she is submitted to the basic contract of saying whatever crosses her or his mind. This contract, if respected, will produce symptoms of hysteria. That is why the analysand is represented in the position of the other as a $, cut from the meaning of his symptoms, and producing a master-signifier from which he is literally barred.

The *o* object represents the other of the analysand, the analyst himself in position of agent; he is the cause of the desire to know (the meaning of the symptoms produced). He will in return teach the analysand what he didn't know he knew (S_2), this "knowledge of the structure that has the position of truth."[35] The task will be to destroy the analysand's identification with the analyst. Whereas the Master's modus operandi was foreclusion and the University's repression, the Analyst's is displacement (*Verschiebung* in Freud) or transference: a love that should come to its end. "Displacement is the most appropriate means to overcome censorship."[36]

This is how and why Lacan can claim for the Psychoanalyst's discourse the seemingly exorbitant privilege of enlightening the discourses of mastery, by shedding light on the way they foreclose (in the Master's case) or repress their truth (in the University's); indeed, only the passage from one discourse to the other makes the emergence of the repressed possible. This passage is grasped in terms of love or transference, and hence is understandable only through theoretical psychoanalysis.[37]

Moreover, whereas the first two discourses make aggregates of individuals (think about what happens in politics, or the "student body," for example), the third one is geared toward the singular: "What depends on the same structure doesn't automatically have the same meaning. That is why you can psychoanalyze only what is singular: an identical structure doesn't come at all from a unique meaning, certainly not when it becomes discourse."[38]

---

35. "Radiophonie, " *Autres écrits*, p. 445.
36. *Écrits*, p. 511.
37. *Séminaire XX*, pp. 20–21.
38. "Introduction à l'édition allémande des *Écrits*," *Autres écrits*, p. 557.

In other words, even if we can classify mental illness by categories, each case, through its singularity, will at some point escape these classifying generalities and show a structure that is unique to the case, or, more radically, something that cannot be taken up in a structural, formalized description: "Clinical types depend on structure, we can write that but not without a certain hesitation. This statement is certain and transmissible only of the hysteric's discourse. That is why a real emerges in it, a real which is close to the scientific discourse. Note that I spoke of the real, and not of nature."[39]

THE HYSTERIC'S DISCOURSE

The clinical type of hysteria would then be the only one that can be fully structured. Again, let us make a last quarter-turn counterclockwise, which will allow us to derive its structure from the Psychoanalyst's discourse and thus reveal the latter's operational truth (see Fig. 3–5).

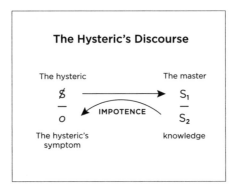

The Hysteric's Discourse

The hysteric   The master

$$\frac{\not{S}}{o} \xrightarrow{\quad\quad} \frac{S_1}{S_2}$$

IMPOTENCE

The hysteric's symptom   knowledge

Figure 3–5.

The barred subject $\not{S}$ (the hysteric) is now in the position of the agent; the o object occupies in his statement the position of the truth he has no access to. He produces knowledge by addressing himself to the other, which is now the master-signifier, or even the master or father themselves. This is how Lacan summarizes the relationship between Freud

---

39. *Ibid.*

and his patient Dora: "The hysteric is the divided subject who drives the master in a corner to force him to produce a knowledge."[40] The reading of another Freudian case (the "beautiful female butcher") is similar: "The hysteric's discourse questions the master: 'Show me if you are a man!' "[41]

On several occasions, Lacan will make of this symptomatic structure the anologue of that of scientific discourse: "Hysteric and scientific discourses have almost an identical structure."[42]

This congruence is based first on a reading of the emergence of the structure of the unconscious. It was by listening to hysterics that Freud first understood that the symptoms they produced were the cipher of a hidden structure, which he then undertook to explore during the rest of his life. The hysterical symptoms were the way (along with dreams) toward the mapping out of the real: "The question is not about the discovery of the unconscious, whose matter is preformed in the symbolic order, but about the creation of the disposition through which the real [as structure] touches on the real [as unconscious], that is the psychoanalytical discourse."[43]

The hysteric's discourse (when listened to by the analyst) hence manifests a real structure; that is why it is very close to science, which deducts from its algorithms the structure of matter.

The difference is that science, per se, as we have seen repeatedly, is not an undertaking preoccupied by the abolition of the subject's truth that its own expansion produces constantly. Hence science is not preoccupied by truth, and it is not true regarding the subject; it is only exact regarding the objects of the world: "To believe that science is true because it is transmissible is a delirious idea."[44] Science is transmissible only because it is exact. By contrast, the hysteric's discourse is for the analysand and the analyst together the way to the truth of the barred subject; the difference between science and hysteria is then nothing other than the difference between the subject's scientific abolition and the subject's hysterical negation through the symptom. Or, in other

---

40. "Radiophonie," *Autres écrits*, p. 436.

41. *Ibid.*, p. 90.

42. "Télévision," *Autres écrits*, p. 523. See also ". . . ou pire," *ibid.*, p. 548, where Lacan speaks of the affinities between hysteria and science.

43. ". . . ou pire," *ibid.*

44. "Note italienne," *Autres écrits*, p. 309.

words, if we remove the myth-making inherent to the discourse of hysteria, we are led to the discourse of science.

A Matrix of the Four Discourses

To conclude, let us underline that the four discourses organize themselves in a matrix. As always in Lacan, it is possible to integrate categories and names to show the algorithm's efficiency and power: just as is the case with the schema L', Lacan's formulas are capable of putting an enormous number of distinct concepts in relation.

To each discourse of the matrix (see Fig. 3–6), we will attribute a clinical classification, a master case, a psychic process, and finally an institution or type of knowledge.

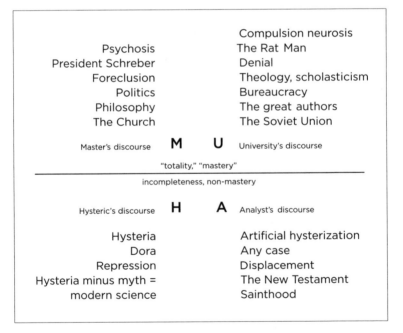

Figure 3–6. The four discourses organized in a matrix.

Making the usual quarter turn will specify the dominant discourse in which the subject will inscribe itself. Of course, by transference, we can speak from any discourse at any given moment. More: "Meaning is produced only by the translation from a discourse into another."[45] We keep in mind here the distinction between signification, which is always imaginary, and meaning, which is real-unconscious. This means that, even as the Master's discourse never stops producing the significations it dearly wishes to bundle into a totality, the meaning and truth of its production can be revealed only by its translation (or transference) through the Analyst's discourse and its raking light. The meaning of any given discourse can be revealed only from the outside of its closed structure.

To give another example of how the general matrix functions, let us choose Catholic religion. Its discourse starts as the Analyst's does, as evidenced by Lacan's take on Christianity as the "true religion." The Church will transform the Gospel into an institution (a task that Saint Paul accomplished), and thus inscribe the Gospel as the sacred and canonical text of reference (it is not by chance that the Church gave birth to our present-day universities in the twelfth century). The Gospel is then commented on by academic scholasticism, which tries to master it. The Church and theology as institutions also try to reduce the saint's claim of accessing God without any help from an institution. By analogy, the analyst as a saint,[46] or as a professional "who is authorized only by himself"[47] to practice psychoanalysis, is neutralized by the University's discourse.

Of course, inasmuch as the Church is also a political institution, it participates in the Master's discourse. And finally, since Christianity is the bedrock of modern science, it can also be formalized through the Hysteric's discourse.

To summarize, Lacan, with the analysis of discourses, produced a very powerful and rigorous instrument; I can only give a glimpse of the possibilities of this formalization here.

---

45. "L'Étourdit," *Autres écrits*, p. 480.
46. "Télévision," *Autres écrits*, p. 520.
47. "Proposition du 9 octobre 1967 sur le psychanalyste de l'École," *Autres écrits*, p. 243.

4

"There Is No Sexual Rapport"

Freud's doctrine on femininity and sexual difference, in its last stage ("Femininity" [1933], in *New Introductory Lectures on Psychoanalysis*, fifth lecture), is truncated. On one hand, women are underdeveloped men, who replicate masculinity on a smaller scale by clinging to a profound narcissism. This is where the truncating lies, since this mimetic reproduction of men by women prevents Freud from thinking through women's difference. On the other hand, women in Freud are also presented as different, not only because, as hysterics, they forged the path to the discovery of the Unconscious, but also because of the "impenetrable darkness" (*Three Contributions* [1905]), or the "enigma" ("Femininity") of which they are the support. This is the side of applied psychoanalysis, where Freud at the end throws up his hands in despair: neither his therapeutic practice nor his begging of the first female analysts in his circle have provided an answer to the question: "What does a woman want? *Was will as Weib? Che vuoi?*"—a question he threw at

Marie Bonaparte, a particularly unqualified person in this respect, in 1928.[1]

This ambivalence (or contradiction) can be further elaborated on the level of theoretical psychoanalysis if we summarize Freud's doctrine about femininity:

1. "There is only one sexuality, phallic in its essence."
2. "We are all bisexual."

Apparently, there is an irreconcilable contradiction between these two statements, but Lacan will make the contradiction the first point of departure of his own doctrine, not without criticizing Freud on a very important point. The beginning of the latter's conception of sexual difference is anchored in biology, from which he tries to elaborate psychic repercussions. Also, in Freud, the discovery of difference by children is dependent on an empirical experience (mainly the discovery by girls and boys alike of the absence of a penis on the female body); what happens if there is no experience of sexuality, no sighting of the mother's or a boy's body? This of course, has to be nuanced by Freud's affirmation, in the chapter "Infantile Sexuality" in *Three Essays on the Theory of Sexuality*, that children's mythology about sex (the phallic mother, for example) is more pertinent to the question than anything adults can elaborate. This constitutes an implicit acknowledgment that sexual difference is not dependent on a pragmatic exploration or a biological difference.

Indeed, the question cannot be asked from an empirical or biological point of view. Hence, we can happily get rid of such Freudian contradictions like *Penisneid*, which is supposedly built by the little girl through an empirical observation of her organ "inferiority," as well as of the biological comparison between male and female sexual appara-

---

1. "What do women want? Freud remains ignorant about an answer to this question to the very end . . ." *Autres écrits*, p. 370. See Paul Verhaeghe's *Does the Woman Exist? From Freud's Hysteric to Lacan's Feminine*; New York: Other Press, 1999, as well as Serge André's *What Does a Woman Want?*; New York: Other Press, 1999, on Freud's and Lacan's discourses on femininity.

tus: "Biological bisexuality (in Freud) has to be left to Fliess's inherit-ance."[2] The problem has to be tackled at the level where the *o* object cannot sustain the unity implied by the sexual act—that is, at the level of language.

Moreover, for Lacan, Freud's failure in front of the "impenetrable" darkness, and the silence of female analysts about feminine sexuality is not the mark of a conceptual impotence or of a mystery beyond de-ciphering (commonly referred to as the "Eternal Feminine"); rather, it has to with a structural question.[3] In other words, the silence or the conceptual fantasies ("clitoral" or "vaginal" orgasm, reduction to phallic jouissance) on feminine sexuality are in themselves a symptom of femi-nine sexuality, to be taken and interpreted as such.

We can infer from Freud's frustration that the question of femininity is an experience; however, *it is an experience for which we lack words*—the quintessence of experience, then. It cannot be easily grasped in a description or an image: femininity is in its essence unconscious. Femininity is therefore what undoes any attempt at theo-rizing it: more generally, femininity is what posits the limits of theoretical psychoanalysis, which makes the practice of psychoanaly-sis, as Lacan had it, a *trick*, of which, in the end, he confessed, he could not explain the workings. In other words, the truncating of Freudian doctrine is structural, and, for Lacan, the occasion for a huge development.

---

2. "La logique du fantasme," *Autres écrits*, p. 325. And: "The relationship of the subject to the phallus is established without consideration of the anatomical differ-ence of the sexes, which makes it particularly difficult to interpret in women and in relation to women," in "*La signification du phallus*," *Écrits*, p. 686. See also "Propos directifs pour un Congrès sur la sexualité féminine," *Écrits*, pp. 727–728. Wilhelm Fliess was Freud's temporary alter ego; he built a theory of sexuality, from which Freud bor-rowed certain elements (see Peter Gay, *Freud, A Life for Our Time*; New York: Norton, 1988, pp. 55–69).

3. "*Our colleagues the women analysts, on feminine sexuality they don't tell us all!* It is really striking. They have contributed nothing at all to the question. To this, there must be an internal reason, tied to the structure of the apparatus of jouissance." *Séminaire XX*, p. 54.

Let us then rewrite the Freudian statements:

1. There is only one sexuality (the phallic one) *that is represent-able*. The Other sexuality exists, but beyond words, or not wholly encapsulated by representation.[4]
   Or: There is one sexuality; then there is an Other one, radically different, an Absolute Other.[5]
2. We are all split (men and women) by sexual difference, but inside ourselves. That is, sexual difference plays itself out not by opposing a female individual to a male individual, but first and foremost by dividing each subject in a singular way. This said, men and women live and dream this inside split in a different manner.

But what is to be understood under the coinage of phallic sexuality? What exactly is the phallus? Not an organ, not a symbol, not a fantasy, not a partial object, but a signifier.[6] As such, it is the object of what Freud called "originary repression," the lone signifier of desire that has been submitted to castration. Hence, in Lacan, not only will any signified (any represented object) be a substitute for the phallus, but also and more importantly, because of the bar of repression that makes it an inaccessible symbol, the whole of sexual dialectics are made excentric regarding the phallus. Lacan's doctrine is not phallocentric, it is phallo-excentric.

As a signifier, the phallus is neither the object of an initiation (as in ancient mysteries and many religions and mythologies), nor a "magic key to dreams and discourses,"[7] but a key item in a language

---

4. "There is a feminine nature only inasmuch as this nature is excluded by the nature of words." *Séminaire* XX, p. 68.

5. "In the phallocentric dialectics, a woman represents the Absolute Other." "Propos . . . ," *Écrits*, p. 732. In other words, phallocentric dialectics is possible only because it has a limit: femininity. It cannot claim to represent the subject without immediately being undone by this limit.

6. "The Signification of the Phallus" (first read in 1958), Ecrits, A *Selection*, p. 285.

7. See the remarks under "phallus," in *Dictionnaire de la psychanalyse*, eds. Roland Chemama and Bernard Vandermersch; Paris: Larousse, 1998.

and a logic of the unconscious. It deploys its effects in the Symbolic order as "equivalent to the logical copula"; in the Imaginary order as the vital flux circulating in the process of generation; and in the Real as a symbol of copulation.[8]

Later, Lacan will deem the phallus to be mythical, in the sense that its function will be to hide the gap between the two genders: "In psychoanalysis (as well as in the unconscious), men don't know anything about women, and vice-versa. The phallus is the only mythical point where sexuality becomes the passion of the signifier."[9]

We can say that Lacan is here faithful to the two axioms of Freud's account of human sexuality: there is only one side (the phallic one) that is representable; there is an Other side that escapes language and cannot be represented in its entirety. The unconscious knows only one representation of desire, the phallus, making the representation of the Other sex impossible; hence a representation of the sexual rapport has always to do with the phallus, and it will always be mythical.

The fact that there is a phallic function organizing signifieds and representations around a missing element, the phallic signifier, doesn't mean that psychoanalysis is phallocentric or even that patriarchy depends on this function. Patriarchy only perpetuates the phallus's imaginary effects. The United States is the only country in the world where Lacan is accused of phallocentrism. In France, Italy, South America, where he has a wide following, this accusation is never leveled at his thought; many women, and many women analysts, have no qualms about being labeled as Lacanians. This is a symptom that needs to be addressed and examined.

From what I know of Lacan's theory, indeed, nothing can justify this accusation, unless the use of the terms "phallus" and "phallocentrism" qualifies you automatically as a "macho" person. Such a view, no doubt, would also assume that anybody who utters the word "racism" is a racist, or, in other words, that we are directly what we say and what we talked about—a move that both psychoanalysis and the theory of enunciation forbid.

---

8. *Écrits* (English), p. 285.
9. "Radiophonie," *Autres écrits*, p. 412.

There is thus a nominalistic phobia of the word "phallus," not of the phallus itself as defined by Lacan; this phobia translates to a penis phobia, but it could also work in reverse as a penis phobia transposed to the phallus. The fetishization of the concept leads to a negative moralization that is not warranted by the theory; moreover, the fact that a phallic function exists doesn't make psychoanalysis phallocentric.

Lacan's insistence on the universality of castration is here sufficient to show the "ex-centricity" of sexual dialectics regarding the phallus. Patriarchy, in this respect, has to be reinterpreted as an imaginary effect of the phallic function.

A first systematic table of this difference can be extracted from "*La signification du phallus.*"

A woman (as a singularity)	Men (as a class)
1. Requests from men to *have* the phallus. ("Give me what you don't have.")	1. Request a woman to *be* the phallus. ("Be what you cannot be [woman as the phallus].")
2. Rejects her femininity to be what she cannot be (the phallus).	2. Want to be the phallus to answer a woman's request.
3. Men in this regard suffer from a lack of *having*.	3. A woman is the site of an ontological lack, a lack of *being.*
4. Looks for an ideal man (a phallic one).	4. Look for yet another woman who could be it (maybe by trying yet another one; imitate Don Juan).
5. A woman is then suffering from a *continuous* disappointment, since the phallic man doesn't exist.	5. Men work under the illusion that they can add to their conquests in order to produce a sum, a totality. This leads them to *repeated* disappointment.

We can readily observe how asymmetrical the requests of the two genders are. They cross over without encountering each other, which is another way to affirm what will later be described by Lacan as the inexistence of the sexual rapport.

Between the two sexes, love and hate will occur through projections and identifications. Even love is but a projection (as Freud had it): the object, the little *o* of love, is always internal to the subject and projected outside; which is to say, love is inherently narcissistic. A common error here is to take the object of our love for something Other than our projections.

In this framework, how can we redefine love? Feminine love is essentially a request to a man to furnish what he does not have (a phallus), and masculine love an asymmetrical request to the woman to be what she cannot be (a phallus). There is no chance that either request can ever meet the other in a happy complementarity.

From Lacan's rewriting of Freud's doctrine, no gender can claim any superiority over the other one. This is because all men have an unconscious—that is, a feminine—"side" (beyond words), and all women speak, so that, inasmuch as they are speaking beings, they are submitted to the phallo-excentric logic. Crucial inferences can be derived from this. In particular, no subject (and no object—speech, images, fantasies—produced by this subject) can be analyzed without reference to its Other side. No woman can be understood without reference to the phallo-excentric logic of language, no man can be grasped without an understanding of the relationship he entertains with the unconscious, that is, femininity. Furthermore, no absolute singularity can be analyzed without reference to the generality that defines it. In this respect, men's, or women's, or queer, or lesbian studies appear hopelessly truncated if they insist on a group's particularity: the consequence being of a deep segregation and the building of autistic ghettos.

In 1973, Lacan proposed a table (see Fig. 4–1) to describe sexual difference. It is to be found in *Séminaire XX*.[10]

---

10. See Bruce Fink's translation, published by Norton, New York (1998), and Juliet Mitchell's and Jacqueline Rose's introductions in *Feminine Sexuality: Jacques Lacan and the École Freudienne*; New York: Norton, 1982.

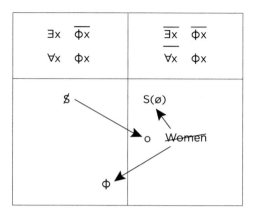

Figure 4–1. Table of sexual difference.

First of all, the headers of the boards have to be explained; they separate the two columns so that the one that is masculine is on the left, the feminine on the right, and the choice of where he or she would be inscribed is independent of biological constraints.[11] The terms are written in the symbols of modern logic. Note that Lacan purposely commits an infraction of the rules in order to write the absence of sexual rapport.[12] Nothing indicates more clearly the difference between science and psychoanalysis than this "distorted" use of mathematics by Lacan, by which he negates that "one exists." Let us take the groups of symbols one by one.

1. $\exists x \overline{\Phi x}$

There is an x (= a human subject) that does not verify the phallic function. This describes the paternal function, the Symbolic father, who, being dead, is evidently beyond castration. Being an exception, he negates the phallic function by constituting the limit beyond which this very function cannot reach.

---

11. "It is possible for any speaking being—with or without the attributes of masculinity—to put itself in this column on the right"; *Séminaire XX*, p. 74.

12. "This writing is not used in mathematics. To negate—as signified by the bar of negation above the quantor—that *one* doesn't exist is not done." *Autres écrits*, p. 465. See Alain Vanier's commentary in *Lacan*; New York: Other Press, 2000, pp. 65–83.

2. $\forall x \, \Phi x$

All x's verify the phallic function, whoever they are: all human beings, inasmuch as they speak, are submitted to castration. This includes, but only partially, those speaking beings who are female.

3. $\overline{\exists x} \; \overline{\Phi x}$

There is no x for which the phallic function is not verified; women, since they speak, are submitted to the phallic function.

4. $\overline{\forall x} \, \Phi x$

It is not for all x's that the phallic function is verified; a woman is the exception to the law of castration (i.e., the phallic function). So the function of limit granted to the dead father now crosses over to a singular woman.

The table's headers render manifest a logical contradiction: each proposition is immediately confronted with its logical negation, and that means that logic is not all-encompassing. ("All universal propositions must be limited by an existence that negates them.")[13]

We can now inscribe human subjects, on the two sides of the table, insofar as they are determined by these logical contradictions.

On the male side, where the phallic function Φ is inscribed, we have a barred subject; it is barred because it has two components: language and not language, representation and an unconscious to which the subject has not direct access. This subject is the support of a vector, where his desire is reduced, alienated, and figured by a request for an o object. This vector alienates itself in a fantasy; in other words, the desire for femininity is captivated by a "reality" that in fact is nothing other than the subject's construct (this is what Freud called the reality principle). Men overcome the limit or border that separates the sexes only through their own fantasies. The signifier of this fantasy (the o object) doesn't catch the Real of femininity in its net, only an imaginary signified (a signification). That is why Lacan can say: "The essence

---

13. "L'Étourdit," *Autres écrits*, p. 451.

of the object is failure."[14] Jouissance (the aim of desire) is grasped only in the dimension of its loss, which is represented by an object that does not encompass desire in its totality. Male (phallic) jouissance alienates desire in the failure of its object.

On the female side, you have barred women, according to the impossibility of making a class of the individual beings that support femininity; hence they have to be taken one by one. From a woman emerge two vectors of desire. One is directed toward the phallic function (it is a desire that requests its representation). Note that the vector doesn't coincide with men's request. It is a request for a purely phallic (ideal) man, which is destined to be frustrated as deeply as are men's requests for a woman to be the phallus. In other words, a woman's desire considers a man only as a support for the phallic function, a consideration that is bound to find its limit in castration.

The other vector directs itself toward femininity as such, a signifier that represents the Other sex, itself being barred (because one part of it cannot access representation). Here, nothing makes sexual difference, and the drama of these requests that can never overlap, more visible; men's desire finds its failure in an o object that is but the truncation of desire, its own alienation (it will always fail to represent the mother adequately). A woman's desire is split between a continuous disappointment (there is no really phallic man, they are all castrated), and a vector that never can find a representative object because of its unconscious nature.

As such, women have to be defined as "not-whole"; they are not entirely defined by phallic jouissance, they are not entirely submitted to the phallic function, and femininity establishes itself beyond the control of these representational effects. We will leave it to the reader to assess if this Lacanian conception of femininity doesn't give feminism a stronger basis than a simple claim to a "male" imaginary position. What is clear, however, is that femininity, in Lacan, is a more real, more powerful entity than all the discourses that attempt to encompass it, and that therefore reduce it. The positioning of femininity as not wholly representable places it on the side of truth (as not entirely utterable) and the unconscious, inasmuch as the latter escapes formalization.

---

14. *Séminaire XX*, p. 55.

We are now able to understand what Lacan means by the lack of sexual rapport.[15] This point needs to be emphasized; as far as the symbolic effects of language on man are concerned, it may perhaps be the ultimate consequence of Lacan's theory. However, the present translation of *rapport sexuel* as "sexual relationship" is an absurdity that leads commentators to strange contortions. If Lacan had meant physical coitus, he would have used the common French expression *relations sexuelles*. Lacan did not intend to deny the existence of sexual relationships (Who would?). When he used *rapport*, he was pointing to the impossibility of construing a *logical* relationship between two *signifiers*, "man" and "woman."

In Lacan, the equivalent of "sexual relationship" is "*l'acte sexuel*"; its function is twofold; first, to reiterate in vain a sexual identity, the belonging to one side or the other of the sexual divide that is threatened by the absence of sexual rapport: "No sexual act is enough to confirm in the subject that he (or she) belongs to one gender only."[16]

Second, repression (in its psychoanalytical sense) is exercised only against sexual acts because, since they fail to prove that we belong to one gender only, they expose in the end the splitting of the subject between phallic and feminine sexualities: "Thought has to defend itself only against sexual acts, because, in them, the subject splits itself."[17]

In other words, the sexual act is the first step toward repression or sublimation (that is why Lacan affirms that no sexual liberation is possible, either through acts or through thinking); conversely, the unity of thought is a fantasy. The sexual act is at the same time the first entry of human sexuality in the domain of the Law. Both its pleasurable failure at uniting the sexes and its finality (which makes it encounter the law of the absence of sexual rapport) explain not only why we like to repeat the sexual act,[18] but also why this repetition is unconsciously and symbolically under the spell of an unavoidable necessity, one that has

---

15. However maladroit, this is the only formulation I have found that doesn't enmesh Anglophone readers in a confusion between sexual relationships (coitus) and the logical problem of rapport as developed by Lacan.

16. "La logique du fantasme," *Autres écrits*, p. 325.

17. *Ibid.*

18. "That is why love is insatiable; its existence depends on the absence of sexual rapport." "L'Étourdit," *Autres écrits*, p. 467.

nothing to do with the urge of an animal instinct. In history, both Roman orgies and ascetic saints in the desert prove the point.

"There is no sexual rapport" is a proposition derived from experience, acquired by the psychoanalyst through the cure, from Freud's writings on the problem and from pure logic. If there is only one symbol to represent bisexuality (the phallus), then the two sides of the equation, male and female, cannot be put into a logical rapport, they cannot be written in a logical formalization:

x Ɍ y (x = a man, R = rapport, y = a woman) is not possible.

There is no completeness, no totality: this is where Lacan markedly differs from the aspect of Freud's thinking that goes back to Plato's hermaphrodite[19] to explain the attraction of one sex for another. The two genders, for Lacan, aim at completing each other only by virtue of an imaginary fantasy (love), or find this "union" only in an intensely frustrating symbolic decision, marriage for example: "All marriages, and not only in neurotics, carry castration with them."[20] The Law will here incarnate a double frustration: the husband will have to forgo his quest for a fantasized "totality" of femininity, realized in sleeping with yet another woman; the wife, disappointed by her non-phallic husband, will have to abandon her quest for the ideal and undiscoverable man who would have the phallus.

The absence of sexual rapport (which is but another name for castration) has meaning only from a real and symbolic point of view; there is an Imaginary relationship between men and women (the fleshy reality to which we can all attest), and there is a Symbolic one, which varies according to customs and laws. But there is no unconscious sexual rapport: in the Real, men and women are condemned to miss each other for eternity (as long as they will speak). The sexual rapport is thus "what never ceases not to be written"[21] in a symbolic way. This constitutes a redefinition of the unconscious: at its core lies

---

19. Freud, *Beyond the Pleasure Principle*; New York: Norton, 1961, pp. 69–70. To explain sexual difference, Greek mythology here lends a hand to biology, which, at this level, is therefore nothing but another mythology.

20. *Séminaire IV*, p. 213.

21. *Séminaire XX*, p. 87.

a void of non-representability that is in itself the lack of sexual rapport. In the reverse, symbolization is an agent of repression: as soon as something is written, it covers up its incompleteness, it avoids the confrontation with the lack that undoes any claim to totality. Lacan expressed this process by a rewording: "The sexual rapport is what ceases, because it is written."[22]

Now, if only phallic sexuality is representable, the Other sex (femininity) is unconscious. If "the speaking being shows sex as such as feminine,"[23] it means that the phallo-excentric dialectics creates a repressed that is really sexual, but unspeakable. That is why Lacan can declare that women are "born psychoanalysts";[24] it implies that men have to learn psychoanalysis, because their relationship to their unconscious is different.

Femininity is always singular; women as a general class don't exist. There is only one woman, then another one, just as there is one singular unconscious, then another one. Constructing a general class including all women is either an Imaginary or a Symbolic act, it has nothing to do with real logic. However, we can build a class of men, inasmuch as they are all submitted to the phallic function, that is, ultimately, inasmuch as they are all defined by castration. This definition applies only partially to women, for the part of them that is engaged in phallo-excentric discourse. Another part is beyond representation—beyond the phallus and phallic jouissance. Hence there is an essential difference between man and woman, in Lacan as well as in Freud.

We can summarize the difference brutally: a woman wants to find the ideal man, a man wants to sleep with all women. In 1956, Lacan affirmed that "In a woman, the ideal of conjugal conjunction is monogamous, because she wants the phallus for her alone. As far as men are concerned, because the typical normative and legal union is always marked by castration, this union tends to the reproduction of the split in him that makes him fundamentally bigamous."[25] What is always emphasized here is the dissymmetry of relationships.

---

22. *Les non-dupes errent.* Unpublished seminar, February 19, 1974.
23. *Autres écrits*, p. 370.
24. *Ibid.*
25. *Séminaire IV*, p. 213.

In Galilean terms (in the universe of modern science), the absence of sexual rapport is both a mental experiment and a crucial one. As opposed to science (where there are only mental experiments), the psychoanalytical encounter—with its absence of sexual rapport—prevents applied psychoanalysis (the cure) from being inscribed completely in modern science: only theoretical psychoanalysis may be submitted to this inscription, and the experience of the void of sexual rapport is the singular limit that resists the generalization implied in its formalization. Psychoanalysis (including the crucial experiment of the cure) cannot be science in its entirety. We can say also that femininity, the Other sex, or the Other of sex, is the crucial experiment that undoes any attempt at verbalizing sexuality as a totality in the world of concepts.

The consequences of this paradigm, which Lacan reaches through a rigorous logical determination, are everywhere.

In mythology, the absence of sexual rapport can be read everywhere in its denial; not only in the Platonic hermaphrodite myth that Freud used,[26] but in all the myths of origin that describe a cosmos born out of the copulation of a female and a male element. In that sense, the denial of the absence of sexual rapport marks all the science of antiquity as mythology up to the point of its demise and substitution by modern science: for example, the theory of the four elements, prevalent in classical and medieval times, makes matter itself a player in the sexual drama; air and fire are masculine, water and earth feminine, and a sturdy chain is needed to bind these opposing forces together. Alchemy, in particular, is entirely understandable as a mythical quest for the harmony of the male and female elements that are the building blocks of the cosmos.[27]

Hence psychoanalysis negates the harmony of speech and thought and the harmony of thought and world that it would depend on.

We still labor very hard under the weight of these mythic motives: witness the success of our pastoral ecology, grounded on the illusory harmony of man and nature, a dream that does not take into account the break by the irruption of language that makes the world a world of words. Witness the strong remnants, in our culture, of the omnipotence

---

26. See p. 98 of this volume. Again, Freud himself is not entirely unencumbered by his own mythology.

27. "Primitive science is a kind of sexual technique." *Séminaire XI*, p. 139.

of thought, as translated in the belief in or the quest for the harmony of thought and world; or witness its variant, the widespread conviction of harmony of thought and speech,[28] based on the denial of an unconscious thought (which is the belief that we can fully "express" what we are, what we want, and what we think); or the belief that there can be harmony between thought and soul.[29] All these motives make up the elements of a modern mythology, the basis of which is the firm belief in a harmony between men and women, the belief in the existence of a sexual rapport. A *contrario*, the absence of sexual rapport is not only an ethical pronouncement, it is a statement belonging to the universe of modern science, inasmuch as this statement undoes the imaginary mythologies of complementarity, harmony, and totality between the two genders, mythologies that are still very much alive today. It is also proof that modern man, as Freud and Lacan always surmised, is still very close to his primitive brethren.

We must emphasize here that the Imaginary order obeys a necessity. That is why, even if it is determined by the Symbolic order, no subordination other than a logical one can be attributed to it; the hierarchy implied by the ordering of the letters *R, S, I,* a pun on "heresy," is an ordering of priorities for the psychoanalyst, not an ethical command. The function of the Imaginary order is to promulgate life through the denial of the absence of sexual rapport and through the libido's investment in objects. As such, this order cannot be dismissed only as alienation: "The mirror image is the channel that libido takes to go from the body to the object."[30] The Imaginary order operates the transformation of libido into objects and images: its purpose is then to perpetuate life, as opposed to the Symbolic order (language) that is the carrier of death and the death drive. Hence, the Imaginary order is life, or life is an imaginary reality: "Is language grounded on something like life? That would be a good question to address to linguists. This question has to be framed by my terms "Imaginary" and "Real," which distinguish two spaces for life [. . .]. Language ties these spaces; it doesn't say

---

28. See *Autres écrits,* p. 158.

29. "Thought is disharmonic in relationship to the soul." "Télévision," *Autres écrits,* p. 512.

30. *Écrits,* p. 822.

anything about a hypothetical "life of language," if only because language carries death."[31]

Lacan traces the complacent acceptance of a belief that thought and soul are equivalents to the Greek *nous*, from which, he points out, the adequacy of a belief in the equivalence of world and soul derives.[32] In other words, a belief in the possibility of sexual rapport belongs to the thought of antiquity, not to the universe of modern science. Let us restate: we cannot get rid of mythology, it permeates our very being. In the last analysis, the universe of modern science is an impoverished context, radically hostile to the subject of desire; in this universe, there is no sexual rapport, no soul, no totality or wholeness, no serenity, no wisdom, no interiority to console us and compensate for our narcissistic wounds. No wonder we still go back to our familiar mythologies—Oedipus, Mother Nature, the Tantric wheel—all the motifs that will give us the solace of a fantasy of harmony.

The absence of sexual rapport allows Lacan to point out that philosophy itself is not devoid of a sexual mythology. A case in point could be the history of what philosophers have thought about the union of the soul and the body, or its corollary the union of form and matter. At the heart of the metaphysics and the philosophy of Antiquity (which let us suspect that it is not that far removed from mythology), in the founding text of Western philosophy, Aristotle's *Metaphysics*, resides a central problem: the union of matter (substance) and form; Aristotle resolves the question by an analogy: matter is feminine, form is masculine, hence their reunion is akin to a successful coitus.[33] To which Lacan responds, "All this stuff about matter and form suggests that old fable on copulation!"[34]

In arts and literature, examples of the absence of sexual rapport and the denial of this absence are countless; we could almost say that literature and the arts are a privileged field whose sole goal is to con-

---

31. "Peut-être à Vincennes . . . ," *Ornicar?* 1, January 1975, p. 4.

32. "Télévision," *Autres écrits*, p. 512.

33. *Metaphysics*, A, 6, 5: "It is obvious that from one material only one table can be made, whereas the artist who applies the form, while being alone, makes several tables. It is the same in the case of the male in relation to the female: the latter one is fecundated by one coitus, but the male impregnates several females: it is an example of the role played by these principles."

34. *Séminaire XX*, p. 102.

sole us for this very absence, or whose sole goal is to deploy their seductions in order to enable us to deny, hide, forget, veil, make acceptable, or repress the encounter with the impossible Real.

Let us follow Lacan and address the case of courtly love (*Séminaire XX*). Lacan first emphasizes that the inaccessible Lady of courtly love has nothing to do with the medieval historical context, in which most often women were no more than men's slaves. Hence, the courtly Lady is the result of a male poetical fantasy; but to what end? "Courtly love is a very refined way to make up for the absence of sexual rapport, by feigning that we are the origin of the obstacle to the sexual rapport."[35] In other words, the courtly poets created the inaccessible Lady to preserve the belief that, beyond her refusal of carnal pleasures, there was the promise of a sexual rapport. This poetic strategy, for them, had the double advantage of eternalizing their desire of completeness through sexual union and, hence, making eternal their desire for poetry as well as the songs supplicating the Lady to concede. And so the courtly poet joins the ranks of everyday men: a speaking being who prolongs life and desire by his refusal to address the void of the unconscious.

---

35. *Séminaire XX*, p. 65.

5

God Is Real

To begin with, Lacan makes a crucial distinction, which is not done in the academic discipline called "history of religions," between Judeo-Christianity (including its avatar Islam and the other religions):[1] "I will not give you a definition of religion (in general), because there is no more a history of religion than there is an art history. Religions, like arts, are a wastebasket category, because they have no homogeneity."[2]

Schematically, what separates the religions of the Book and the others is their respective positioning on the question of the lack of sexual rapport. The three religions of the Book, it can be said, put this question at their center, without glossing over it. We need not seek further for an example than the Gospels, where, quite literally, Mary has no sexual rapport with Joseph in the procreation of Jesus. The other religions, by contrast, do gloss over it by ultimately choosing to dream about a harmony between men and women and between

---

1. Buddhism is another problem, insofar as it recognizes desire by trying to erase it.
2. *Séminaire XX*, p. 103.

mankind and the world. In other words, Judeo-Christianity has a link to the psychoanalytic truth of the unconscious, whereas other religions can be classified as mythologies that create the dream of a sexual complementarity: their truth has to be measured against the fantasy of a sexual harmony. This dream derives from what Freud called the "omnipotence of magical thought."[3] In other words, mythologies project into the cosmos (myths of origin) a remedy for the lack of sexual rapport; Judeo-Christianity is the opposite, the "true religion,"[4] insofar as it directly deals with this lack. Let us note that we are far from done with the omnipotence of magical thought: it would be an illusion to believe that modern humankind is done with dreaming about (and of) a complementarity, and hence a wholeness, of the opposite sexes.

A brief reminder of Freud's position on these problems is in order:[5]

1. God doesn't exist (hence there is no doctrine of God possible; Freud's scientism on this point opposes him to Lacan, for whom God exists, hence a Lacanian doctrine of religion is possible). The opposition, in Freud, between the (proclaimed) scientificity of psychoanalysis and the illusion of religion is remarkably stable.[6]
2. Religion *is* analogous to a compulsion neurosis in its insistence on repeated ritual acts.
3. The Catholic Church is the non-primal herd of the brothers and sisters in Christ: it is founded on the murder of the Son (repeated by the cannibalistic ingestion of the host), not the murder of the Father as in *Totem and Taboo*.
4. Religion *functions* as a psychosis (it is coherent): "It implies a system of illusion coupled with a denial of reality."[7]

Hence, for Freud, there is a veiled kernel of truth in religion (it is an illusion, not an error). From this illusion, we can obtain truths, not

---

3. In *Totem and Taboo*.

4. *Séminaire XX*, pp. 98 and 102, and *Les non-dupes errent*, unpublished seminar, December 11, 1973.

5. I follow here François Regnault's incisive book, *Dieu est inconscient*; Paris: Navarin, 1985.

6. See Octave Mannoni, "L'athéisme de Freud," in *Ornicar?* 6, p. 21 ff.

7. Freud, *The Future of an Illusion*; New York: Norton, 1989, Chapter VIII.

about a philosophical truth in the world, but about the subject's relationship to the unconscious, sexuality, or taboos.

5. Religious mythology veils the destiny of drives; or, drives produce a religious mythology. Hence, this mythology can be interpreted as if it were a case, since "the theory of drives is so to
   speak our mythology. Drives are mythical beings, imposing in
   their indetermination."[8]
6. Theology is not important (it is a discourse that reinforces the
   religious illusion by rationalizing it; hence it repeats religion).
7. Christianity is but a late Judaism.

In brief, Freud's positions about religion are a scientism, one that is
grounded in a Darwinian theory of evolution. This is perfectly apparent in the myth of the primal herd (in *Totem and Taboo*) as well as in
his reading of the consumption of the Eucharist as a cannibalistic (i.e.,
magical) act. In other words, all religions, including Judeo-Christianity,
are a mythology furthered by a theology: whether it is the return of the
repressed or the return of the dead father, the ritual is the price to pay
for originary guilt.

Lacan, quite to the contrary, centers his approach on an analysis
of creationism. Whereas he accepts Darwin as correct as far as the life
sciences (and nature) are concerned, he rejects any metaphorical translation of Darwinism into the cultural field. This is coherent with "In
the beginning was the Word," which is the basis of his approach to all
human manifestations.

Furthermore, culture is submitted to epistemological breaks that
are created by speech; it is not a field to which natural evolution may
be applied. This is because, at a very general level, the human subject
and his desire cannot exist without a verbal creation: "The notion of
creation *ex nihilo* is coextensive with the exact situation of the Thing
[the mother, the cause of desire] as such."[9]

In cultural matters, evolutionism has little explanatory power;
transposed to the realm of culture, evolutionism is therefore a form of

---

8. Freud, *New Introductory Lectures on Psychoanalysis*, Fourth lecture, p. 130. New
York: Norton, 1965.
9. *Séminaire VII*, p. 147.

religious belief, whose ultimate goal and effect is to reinsert man in nature: "In the beginning was the Word, which means the signifier. Without the signifier at the beginning, it is impossible to articulate the drive as historical. And this is enough to introduce the dimension of the *ex nihilo* in the structure of the psychoanalytical field."[10]

Evolution applied to human culture is then interpreted as a form of defense and denial against cultural epistemological breaks; its continuity is a reassuring solace, not only against ruptures in human history, but also against the division of the subject itself. Evolution masks the subject's split by assuming a harmonious totality grounded in consciousness alone: "The idea of creation is consubstantial to your thinking. You, and everybody, can think only in creationism terms. Evolutionism, of which you believe that it is the most familiar model of your thought, is for you, as for all your contemporaries, a form of defense, of holding on to religious ideals; these prevent you from seeing what is happening in the world surrounding you."[11]

Cultural creationism is then the only perspective that permits the possibility of getting rid of these "religious ideals," of radically eliminating God,[12] because cultural evolutionism always presupposes the intention of a creator-god—that is, a finality to evolution: "There is nothing that can be done against evolutionism; mankind will continue to believe it is the summit of creation: it is the fundamental belief that makes it a religious being."[13] Cultural creationism, which locates creation only in the signifier (language), makes the world a man-made object through the representations created by verbal creations.

All this means, once again, that we have to reject the use of metaphors transposed from the natural sciences when we inquire about human culture: their transfer from that sphere to culture will always result in obfuscation and denial.

Cultural creationism implies that there are discontinuities in the history of human thought, moments where something radically new emerges. Following Lacan, and his masters Alexandre Koyré and Alexandre Kojève, we can propose a theory of epistemological cuts, as Jean-

---

10. *Séminaire VII*, p. 252.
11. *Ibid.*, p. 152.
12. *Ibid.*, p. 253.
13. "Petit discours à l'ORTF," *Autres écrits*, p. 222.

Claude Milner has done,[14] and prolong the remarks made in the chapter devoted to epistemology. Indeed, the cuts are easily localizable in the "paradigm shift," as Thomas Kuhn has it,[15] such as the one that occurred when Copernicus, Kepler, and Galileo created modern science. A major epistemological break is a break of such a kind that the names before the cut and the names (even the identical ones) after it cannot be synonymous—they are homonymous. As an example of homonymy, consider the word *orb* before Kepler and after him; even if sounding the same, it doesn't designate the same object at all. Before, it is the perfectly round circumference traced by a planet on a sphere of crystal, which rubs against the other adjacent spheres and thus produces the music of the cosmos. These conceptions of spherical perfection and musical harmony no doubt have a powerful psychological effect, which at the same time explains them: the mankind of antiquity is convinced it is at the center of the cosmos and lives in harmony with its surroundings. After the epistemological cut, after Kepler, *orb* is an irregular ellipsis whose only material existence is a mathematical formula. Another example would be *momentum*, or movement in Aristotle and Galileo. We can therefore collapse the theory of epistemological cuts with the theory of homonyms: they are one and the same.

The positioning of psychoanalysis in the history of epistemological cuts is for Freud crystal clear: he compared his discovery to the Copernican revolution. Lacan underlines the mythical nature of Freud's reference to Copernicus. Indeed, the existence of the unconscious lowers humankind's claim to be the master of its own house in a way that goes beyond Copernicus's heliocentrism, which could not undo the conception antiquity had about a spherical cosmos revolving around a center. The origin of that particular upheaval of our vision has to be traced back to Kepler. Beyond this historical point, for Lacan, psychoanalysis is not a revolution (a movement that allows for a repositioning of concepts or functions without affecting the fundamental structure), but an extension of modern science.[16] It is therefore not a major epistemological

---

14. In Milner's major article, "Lacan and the Ideal of Science," in *Lacan and the Human Sciences*, pp. 27–42.

15. See in particular Kuhn's *Structure of Scientific Revolutions*; Chicago: University of Chigaco Press, 2nd ed., 1970.

16. "Radiophonie," *Autres écrits*, pp. 420–431.

cut, contrary to what Freud asserts, but a subcut inside the field created by Galilean science. Psychoanalysis does not claim to be a revolution. It proposes a different angle of approach to existing structures of thought, although this is a move that may be more subversive than upheavals that labor under the illusion that they are destroying the past while they repeat it.

Homonymization, the process that creates homonyms, allows for the distinction of major and minor cuts, or even the nonexistence of some movements that are presented as cuts. The concept of the Renaissance springs to mind. What I find in the Renaissance are a lot of synonyms inherited from the Middle Ages, but no homonyms; hence the Renaissance is not a major cut. Indeed, the major accomplishment of the Renaissance is an evolution and a transference; that is, the same reverence manifested by medieval theologians for the letter of the Gospels is now applied to Greek and Roman pagan literature. So what we oppose to theology and the Church and call humanism is in fact an outgrowth of these two medieval institutions. Postmodernism comes to mind too; it is perhaps a subcut, but according to my criteria not a major one.

But are there moments of homonymization that change everything, all the names? Note that I don't say that no old names will survive. But precisely, the old names will be survivors, relics, testimony to the world that has disappeared; or, if you want, the old names will now testify to our reluctance to relinquish our old ways. For indeed we do like continuity, it is in itself reassuring, and we don't like cuts, especially major ones; in fact we abhor them because they are inherently threatening. The fact of the matter is that cuts are most often accompanied by a violence that is sometimes without limits; martyrs of a new religion, victims of religious war or of political terror, and the thinning of the subject of desire by the subject of science are all testimonies to this violence.

Cuts are also very apparent in the history of religion, and we can readily account for their effects on the subject. In this framework, a major moment of homonymization occurs at the creation of Judaic monotheism and its rejection of idolatry, against all the mythologies that surrounded the Jews in the ancient Middle East. The multiple gods of the Babylonian, Sumerian, and Egyptian theologies are rejected in favor of a unique God. Moreover, this God is no longer conceived as residing inside the cosmos. Through the dogma of creation *ex nihilo*, He is outside of our world, transcendent to our cosmos. Hence, even if Judaism uses the same names for its divinity as the surrounding mythologies (*El*, for example), the signified and meaning of this name has been radically altered: the new God is homonymous to the old ones. One very important consequence of Judaism's epistemological cut, its radical iconoclasm, is to make purely abstract thought possible; furthermore, for Lacan this iconoclasm provides the appropriate conditions for the discovery of the unconscious by Freud: "This is due only to Freud's Jewish tradition, which is a literal tradition that ties him to science, and, by the same token, to the Real."[17]

The same reasoning applies of course to the gods of Greek and Roman mythology, and can be extended to the philosophical domain; whatever the merits of Greek science and philosophy, it always thinks of itself as inside an uncreated world of objects; indeed, Aristotle's unique God in the *Metaphysics* is still a substance; only the Platonic eternal idea is close to the Creator God of Judaism. But Plato's discourse too remains enclosed in a realm of uncreated matter: in other words, there is a firm limit to abstraction in Greek thought.

This leads to the further epistemological cut that depends on Jewish monotheism, namely, the Incarnation; this is the only dogma specific to Christianity, its only real and radical innovation. Here we have a discourse, whose clearest exposé is in Saint John's Gospel, that makes the abstract and nonrepresentable God of Judaism a man as well. Indeed, the word "god" has once again been homonymized, in a way that is scandalous for the Jews (since God is suddenly in this world) and a folly for the Greeks and, more generally, for mythological thought (since, unlike Jesus, gods in Greek mythology don't have a real body, and thus for a God to be within human flesh would be a symptom of a degradation). This new homonym, Jesus, forces us to consider our body as the incarnation of our drives; no longer can we, as the ancients did, escape our flesh and project into the cosmos the unconscious forces that define our being, or attribute our drives to some external force, to some god or goddess of love, of desire, of war.

But the Incarnation also has something to do with the genealogy of Galilean science. This is true for Lacan as well as for Alexandre Kojève, from whom this link between Catholicism and modern science

---

17. "R S I," *Ornicar?* 5, 1975–1976, p. 43.

is directly derived:[18] "Modern science, created by Galileo, grew only out of Biblical and Judaic ideology, not of the philosophy of Antiquity and Aristotelian conceptuality."[19]

What the new name of God (Jesus) means here is the collapsing of spheres that were separated in both Judaism and Greek mythology: on one side, the supralunar world, the heavens, eternal ideas—eternity, abstraction, pure mathematics, order; on the other, the sublunar world, the earth, change, matter, empirical reasoning, disorder. This was already obvious in the sixth century for a philosopher like Boethius: "The name of Christ is a homonym (aequivocus) and cannot be comprehended by any definition."[20] Boethius's treatise is the point of the departure of the quarrel about universals; he takes sides firmly in the camp of the realists, a position Lacan repeats by affirming that his theory comes from Medieval realism.[21]

When Galileo creates modern science, he does so in reference to an Incarnational framework. Only after Galileo are mathematization (which belonged to the heavens and had very little to do with the human sphere) and empirical verification (which belonged to the world of human activity) reunited. The sublunar and the supralunar worlds are now one: we no longer live in a limited, spherical and material cosmos with its two levels barely connected, we live in a unified universe without limits: we now live, thanks to Galileo, in modernity.

Thanks to Galileo, but also thanks to Jesus Christ, who was the first to have the idea of the collapsibility of the two worlds. Indeed, modern science can arise only in a mental framework that is Christian, even if, after this initial moment, the religious reference is jettisoned by the progress of science. Galileo himself always protested that he was a good Christian, and he was right; concurrently, the Church, which apprehended this new science through the lens of Greek science (that

---

18. See Kojève's "L'origine chrétienne de la science moderne," in Mélanges Koyré; Paris: Hermann, 1964. Lacan acknowledges Kojève as his master: "the freest man I have known," Autres écrits, p. 497.

19. Séminaire VII, p. 147.

20. "Contra Nestorium et Eutychen," in The Theological Treatises; Cambridge, MA: Harvard University Press, 1978, p. 96.

21. "La logique du fantasme," and "De la psychanalyse dans ses rapports avec la réalité," Autres écrits, pp. 327 and 351.

is, Aristotle updated by Saint Thomas Aquinas, i.e., scholasticism), inadvertently sided with a mental framework inherited from paganism when it condemned Galileo. This ironic twist of events is not the only one, since Galileo, at the beginning, set out to give scientific activity the same elevated status that was accorded during antiquity and the Renaissance to what were then called the liberal arts.

Why are there seventeen centuries between the Incarnation and its consequence, modern science? Or (but this is the same question): why are there thirteen centuries from the invention of monotheism to the God Incarnate? I have a simple answer to these questions: psychologically, mentally, and historically we human beings need time to understand. We need to muddle through—sometimes for centuries—to come to the moment where we say: "Aha, this was what was meant by that statement."

Human history is like a huge sentence that has no conclusive punctuation at the end. When I say "I love you" to somebody, I provoke an anticipation and a retroaction that need time to develop and make the meaning of what I say clear; the anticipation begins with the first word: "I," which anticipates what this "I" is about to do. Then the verb "am," which creates another anticipation, then "the God incarnate," the object that resolves the anticipation. Then, by retroaction, my interlocutor and I can begin to build the meaning of the statement; the sentence is reread backwards in order to make sense. It is only when the sentence is complete that the double processes of anticipation and retroaction can come to the provisional closure of signification, truth and/or meaning.

It takes a long time, then, for the consequences of the Incarnation to be drawn (and also an exceptionally gifted individual, Galileo). The dogma of the Incarnation was premature, too strong an anticipation to bear all its fruits at the same time. It's necessary to have Galileo's retroactive comprehension and reception for this dogma to bear its fruits in science. Of course, this process is closely related to the graph of desire (see Chapter 1) and to what Lacan says about "Logical time and the assertion of anticipated certitude."[22] In the case of the Incarnation, seventeen centuries are necessary, as opposed to seconds, minutes, hours, or years in the case of an "I love you."

---

22. *Écrits*, pp. 197–213.

In contrast to Freud's views there is a doctrine of God in Lacan; it is not a dogma, but a set of propositions that can be verified, and modified if necessary, from a reading of the texts produced by Judeo-Christianity.

1. "Religion is true. It is truer than neurosis [. . .], it says that God exists, that He is preeminently existence; i.e., He is repression in itself."[23] Lacan corrects Freud ("God is the return of the repressed") by stating that God is a *content* of the unconscious, not something that emerges through a sublimation, a fantasy, or an illusion, again against Freud's theses in *The Future of an Illusion*. Indeed, the second commandment formulates the impossibility of representing God as an interdiction, which is parallel to the psychoanalytic stance about an unconscious being beyond representation, words, or any formalization. As such, the Judeo-Christian concept of God is correlated to the kernel of the unconscious, the absence of sexual rapport: "God is nothing else than the fact that there is no sexual rapport in language."[24] He is then real, because He signifies the abyss between man and woman: "God is nothing else than that which makes a rapport between sexualized beings impossible."[25]

We may add that Freud, who saw religion functioning as a psychosis, reduced it to the Master's discourse, which assumes that totalization is possible; but, since God as real makes a hole in religious discourse (He is not representable), He escapes the mastery of any discourse, and Freud's definition of religious functioning as psychosis does not describe religion accurately.

2. Science and religion are not opposed as truth and illusion are, but like exactitude and truth, inasmuch as Judeo-Christianity is the "true religion."
3. Only theoretical psychoanalysis is able to redraw this relation of science as exact and religion as true: "The rationalism that

---

23. *Ornicar?* 2, p. 103.
24. *Ibid.*
25. *Ibid.* 2, p. 103.

structures theological thought is not a fantasy—contrary to the platitudes of public opinion."[26]

4. Theology is not a myth (as in Freud) but a structure of knowledge: "Christian truth, in its unsustainable formulation of a God at the same time One and Three, is not beyond a scientific treatment."[27] Therefore, the question of God has to go through the structures of religion, theology, and the Church, which are illusions only when Freud compares them to natural sciences. For Lacan, they face their own truth (they are not mythological).

5. Lacan opposes Freud, who views compulsive neurosis as sufficient to define religions: "It is conceivable that a compulsive neurotic cannot make sense of another compulsive neurotic's discourse. It is from there that religious wars begin: if it is true that, as far as religion is concerned, compulsive neurosis is present, it is the only characteristic that makes religions a class, a characteristic that remains insufficient."[28] To maintain that compulsion neurosis can define religion is to submit religion to the University's discourse, or to see in it only scholasticism and rites, whereas the Analyst's discourse is necessary to grasp it.

6. Theology forces us to think its formulations through: God's death on the Cross, the creation *ex nihilo*, the Incarnation, and more.

Up to a point then, religious discourse and the Analyst's discourse are homologous. The Real (unconscious) in Lacan and God in theology both escape formalization in the same way: they are both impossible to name. In theology, this impossibility of naming God is known as apophatic or negative theology. Both God and the unconscious are Other, escaping the subject's consciousness and conscious speech. The analyst is either a cornerstone,[29] as is Christ in the Bible,[30] or a saint: he is the litter of jouissance;[31] both the saint and the psychoanalyst

---

26. *Écrits*, p. 873.
27. *Ibid*.
28. "Introduction à l'édition allemande des *Écrits*," *Autres écrits*, p. 557.
29. *Séminaire XVII*, p. 125.
30. 1 Peter 2:6, 8.
31. "Télévision," *Autres écrits*, p. 520.

accept being wastebaskets for the symbolic residue of a society, for what a society or a church cannot tolerate openly or even repress (desire in psychoanalysis, direct access to God, bypassing the Church in Catholicism).

The three instances, Real, Symbolic, and Imaginary, are an "infernal Trinity."[32] In Romans 7:7, Saint Paul indicates the dialectical relationship between the Law and sin; Lacan applies it directly to the relationship between the Symbolic order and the Thing of desire, by replacing sin with the Thing: "Is the Law the Thing? God forbid. Nay, I had not known the Thing, but by the Law: for I had not known lust, except the Law had said: 'Thou shalt not covet.'"[33]

Is psychoanalysis, then, an avatar of Catholicism, with the analyst functioning like a priest? Not in the least; indeed, by replacing sin by the Thing, that is, the Mother as forbidden aim of desire, Lacan produces the homonymization of Christian discourse. In Judeo-Christianity, God is conceived as radically out of this world (whose Creator He is), and the religious man "abandons to God the onus of being the Cause."[34] In psychoanalysis, the Cause can be nothing but the unconscious. It is also external, but to man only. So we go from a transcendent exteriority to the world (God as conceived by the Bible and the Koran) to an immanent exteriority in man and in language (the materiality of the symbolic order). Hence, God is radically humanized (anthropomorphized); He cannot exist without being repressed by human language. God is thus inscribed in the symbolic-unconscious axis. Through this inscription, Lacan proposes a radical (and the only logical, I would add) form of atheism: "The true formula of atheism is not that God is dead—even in founding the origin of the father's function on a murder, Freud protects the father—the true formula of atheism is that God is unconscious."[35]

The words are carefully chosen. Lacan doesn't say God is *the* Unconscious: that would be to return to religion, as the one Jung operated; Lacan affirms only that He is part of the human unconscious, a formation thereof. As such, He cannot be an object of faith or belief; Lacan

---

32. *Ornicar?* 4, p. 103.
33. *Séminaire VII*, pp. 101 and 201.
34. *Écrits*, p. 872.
35. *Séminaire XI*, p. 58.

did not want to found a new "religion of the unconscious" or to "liberate" the forces residing in it.

This is a radical anthropomorphization of Judeo-Christianity, whose ultimate consequence is an equally radical atheism. There is only one transcendence left in Lacan, the transcendence of "lalangue," just as there is only one radical exteriority: the exteriority of the symbolic-unconscious axis.

This means, however, that God, faith, and belief are never absent in the modern world, only that they have to be interpreted in psychoanalytic terms. Furthermore, Lacan's doctrine on God makes clear why contemporary atheism, defined by Nietzsche's cry, "God is dead!," is not operative: God is indeed always already dead, hence no declaration will kill Him; He always survives in the form of the unconscious dead father, under the symbolic Name-of-the-Father, hence He doesn't know about the news of his death: "God is dead [. . .] But He doesn't know it. By hypothesis, He will never know it, since He has been dead since the beginning of time."[36] In fact, reasserting His death, as atheism does, is akin to reaffirming His existence.

God is the real figure (not reachable by an act) that prohibits desire and thus preserves it: "The myth that God is dead—I am much less certain about this myth than most contemporary intellectuals, which is not a declaration of theism or of faith in resurrection—this myth is maybe only a shelter against the threat of castration."[37] Furthermore, not without irony, Lacan notes that killing God doesn't resolve any problem, since all the onus of responsibility and guilt is now on the shoulders of humankind.

We can deduce from this that we cannot be an atheist by affirming or wishing to be one. First, belief and faith are implied in these statements, so that they only would be a logical loop (a leap of faith) by which you would ask your audience to believe in what you say, one implying also an act of faith that identifies what you say you are with what you are (an impossibility because of the split nature of the subject).

---

36. *Séminaire VII*, p. 217. Let us underline that God's death, for Lacan, transforms Him into a mythological being, created by the Son, who died *as God* on the Cross and resurrected. (*Ibid.*, p. 209.)

37. *Séminaire VII*, p. 29.

Second, the declaration of God's death doesn't even scratch His unreachable exteriority.

Here we have to distinguish between two gods, following Blaise Pascal, who separates "the God of Abraham and Isaac from the God of the philosophers." The two are the God of religion (Galileo's and Lacan's), who defines real meaning as not representable, as opposed to the God of Aristole, scholasticism, and Descartes, who makes a philosophical construction possible and is therefore an indispensable function of human reasoning. The first god is a god of belief: it is the one whose existence Galileo and Einstein presuppose in order to make science begin or progress; their new understanding of nature works only if a act of faith is its initial moment, by which they assume that God and nature are not fallacious, as in "God does not trick us": if our experiments don't work, it is because our calculations are wrong, not because nature intended to deceive us. It is this God of belief that Lacan aims at when he denies his listeners' atheism: "I defy all of you: I can prove to you that you believe in God's existence."[38] This god is also the god of cultural creationism, the one who says "in the beginning was the word" and who underlies the birth of the symbolic-unconscious order as a radical creation.

Hence, this God, as real, has something to do with psychoanalysis, especially when the latter goes over the bar separating the signifier and the signified to ponder a statement's meaning; "'Meaning is always religious."[39] Faith permeates our everyday life each time we try to attribute to a signified, imaginary signification a real, unconscious meaning, through alienation, repression, foreclusion, or sublimation: "Belief is always the acting out of semblance."[40]

Analysis, in this respect, works as the inversion of belief: "Psychoanalysts have the experience of the fundamental alienation in which any belief sustains itself [. . .] When the signification of belief seems to completely fade away, the being of the subject comes to the light of what was the truth of this belief."[41] For example, when an "I love you"

---

38. *Ornicar?* 5, p. 43.

39. "Lettre de dissolution," *Autres écrits*, p. 318.

40. "Discours à l'Ecole freudienne de Paris," *Autres écrits*, p. 281.

41. *Séminaire IX*, p. 238. See also "The psychoanalytical act would be the act that does not tolerate semblance" in "Discours à l'Ecole freudienne de Paris," *Autres écrits*, p. 280.

shows itself as a "In fact, I love my mother, therefore I hate you because you cannot be her," then love shows the grounding it finds in the alienating belief of the amorous choice. Love is in fact the symptom of the permanence of religious belief in man, the enduring remnant of the omnipotence of thought in modern humankind (see "the overestimation of the love object" in Freud, *Three Essays on the Theory of Sexuality*).

This does not mean that the analyst should behave as a confessor and redirect the analysand's love, by sublimation, toward its proper object, be it God, a lawful spouse, or toward the analyst himself, taken as a paragon of humanity. The task of the analyst is to make the truth of belief understandable, and then make the alienating hiatus between object and desire bearable; central to this task is the destruction of identifications and projections that the analysand makes on his or her analyst through transference.

Furthermore, theoretical psychoanalysis "is not a religion. It proceeds from the same status as science. It is engaged in the central lack where the subject experiences desire."[42] The recourse to mathematical formalization is the major point where theoretical psychoanalysis confirms its radical heterogeneity to religion and theology: "The stability of religion derives from the fact that meaning is always religious. Hence my obstinacy in my way of mathemes."[43] The mathemes—that is, an integral and formalized transmission—are what should prevent psychoanalysts from automatically rebuilding a Church when they group themselves in an association.

Building on Lacan's theory of religion, we can try to introduce some mathemes in Judeo-Christianity to better understand it.[44]

First of all, we have to determine how to write "God"; and there are no reasons, here, to stray from the instructions of thought contained in the books. In the Old Testament, we are commanded not to fabricate any image of God (Moses' second commandment); in the Christian tradition, we have a duplication of the second commandment of Moses, in the form of apophatic or negative theology (it is not possible to form for ourselves an adequate notion, or figure, or word of God).

---

42. *Ibid.*, p. 239.

43. "Lettre de dissolution," *Autres écrits*, p. 318.

44. I am indebted here to Dr. Amadou Guissé, who guided me in the ways of Christian mathemes.

Let us apply the algorithm of the proper name to God, as follows:

$\dfrac{-I}{s}$ = S where $-I$ = the signifier of God

because God is not part of the {0,1} set that defines the concatenation of the signifier. Again, the bar doesn't represent a division (it would be psychosis to consider it as such); we are working here in algebra. In the perfect case where the signified coincides with meaning (s = S), and as such is unpronounceable (Jewish tradition and the Kaballah have fascinating speculations about this theme), I propose this writing for the name of God:

$\dfrac{-I}{S}$ = S, and thus $S \times S = \sqrt{-I}$

Here, you recognize i, the imaginary number mathematicians use, which exists but cannot be represented. Whether in the case of a human subject (see Chapter 1), or God, there is an attribute of existence that is unconscious, and thus unrepresentable. The bar of the quotient, as we have seen previously, is not really a division; it functions like a real border, as an abstract limit of and a relationship between two sets.

Let us now apply the writing of God's name to Christianity. Christianity claims to have the only incarnated god in all history: "In the beginning was the Word, and the Word was with God, and the Word was God [. . .]. And the Word was made flesh, and dwelt among us, full of grace and truth."[45] Here again, we are extremely close to Lacan, who repeats time and again this "In the beginning was the word"; so close that there is no difference to be made, on this point, between the anthropology of Christianity and psychoanalysis.

The algorithm of Christianity may be written thus (Christ being identical to God through the Trinitarian dogma):

j (i) = X, where j = faithful representation, i = God, X = Christ (as exact representation of God)

From the formula of the Incarnation, we can infer the radical singularity of every human subject. It should work like that:

---

45. John 1:1.

X (Christ) = j (i) = j' (i) + ij" (i) where j' (i) is the real part, and j" (i) is the imaginary part[46]

Christian discourse, as formalized, has an impact on sexuality; and, dialectically, Lacan's algorithms formulas have an impact on how we should think about theology and religion.

First of all, if any subject is completely distinct from any other, there is no sexual rapport:

x R̶ y where x = any man, and y = any woman, and R = symbolic relation

The proof resides in the fact that the relation is faithful, hence any two distinct objects having the same image by the representation would be identified as identical. And vice versa, any two distinct representations would be coming from two distinct objects.

The New Testament, viewed through the oblique view of psychoanalysis, inverts the logical chain, if we adhere strictly to its letter. The book says:

1. (Cause) There is no sexual rapport (between Mary and Joseph, a literal statement).
2. (Consequence) Hence there is an incarnated God.
3. (Corollary) Subjects have to be taken one by one.

Logic and psychoanalysis would say:

1. (Cause) There is an Incarnated God.
2. (Consequence) Hence, there is no sexual rapport.
3. (Corollary) Subjects have to be taken one by one.

In psychoanalysis, the Incarnation is the cause of the absence of sexual rapport, whereas, as we learn in Sunday school, the Bible literally makes of this absence (Joseph and Mary didn't sleep together) the cause of the Incarnation.

Of course, humanity has known about the absence of sexual rapport since it began to speak; witness, for example, Leroi-Gourhan's work

---

46. Here, j (i), the image of i by the representation, is not a number, but rather a relation (function) between numbers. The properties verified by j (i) are transported to j' (i) and j" (i) by simple algebra.

on prehistoric art.[47] But Christianity is the first religion to make this absence the epicenter of its discourse.

On the level of (symbolic) sexuality, love is convinced that there is a sexual rapport. Both the Gospel and Lacan fracture this conviction as an illusion. Any x, says love, is in relation with an y, and vice versa. But this happens only through a representation (the imaginary order) that masks the fact that the relation itself is not faithful to its object. In psychoanalysis, this is called projection and identification, without which one would be literally impotent.

The modern subject, which is not only a particularity (an individual who is *part of* an imaginary community, ethnic group, gender, nation, etc.) but an unconscious singularity (which of course brings all kinds of dejection, and objections with it) can be said to have been born in the cradle of Christian discourse.

This seemingly abstruse demonstration allows us to understand more precisely the relationship between Christianity and psychoanalysis, with the caveats mentioned above.

Not only is Christianity the prerequisite to modern science and psychoanalysis as a modern science, it is the unavoidable condition required in order to affirm the absolute (nonmythical) singularity of all subjects, since the Incarnation is the basis for this singularity.

The Christian ethic of love is the necessary corrective to the affirmation of singularity. Without it, the result would be the total war of all subjects against all subjects, each wanting to impose its own desire and singularities. Lacan has noted the step of universal love as one before which Freud always recoils: the commandment to "love thy neighbor" exists to force us to embrace the hatred we have inside us for ourselves and for him.[48] For his part, Lacan proposes his impossible ethics of singularity and desire. The Christian "Love thy neighbor" and the Lacanian "Don't make concessions about thy desire" are therefore at the opposite ends of the ethical spectrum. The "Love thy neighbor as thyself" represents the maximum extension of the ethics of the common good, an extension that takes root in primary narcissism in order

---

47. André Leroi-Gourhan, *Treasures of Prehistoric Art*; New York: Abrams, 1980.
48. *Séminaire VII*, pp. 218–219.

to overcome it. Christian ethics leaves open the question of self-love, which can turn easily into self-hatred. At the opposite end of the spectrum, the Lacanian commandment tries to preserve the uniqueness of each individual, singular desire. Whereas Christian ethics proposes a solution for social woes, Lacanian psychoanalysis limits its focus to the well being of individuals.

Conclusion

Let us imagine a universe where applied psychoanalysis (the cure) as such has disappeared. As I already indicated, Lacan indeed made such a forecast: "It is when psychoanalysis will have been vanquished by the growing impasses of our civilization (a discontent which Freud foresaw) that the indications of my *Écrits* will be taken up again. But by whom?"[1]

Lacan's prognostication is parallel to Freud's pessimistic view of progress, where modernity imposes on humankind ever more impossible tasks, and where the expansion of the superego goes uncontrolled. This would be a world where the unstoppable expansion of science has reached its limits, extenuating or thinning the subject's singular desire through a play of letters and algorithms.[2] Indeed, we may ask if theoretical psychoanalysis as built by Lacan is not a major contributor to the demise of applied psychoanalysis, inasmuch as Lacan's

---

1. "La psychanalyse, raison d'un échec," *Autres écrits*, p. 348.
2. I follow here J.-C. Milner, "Lacan and the Ideal of Science," in *Lacan and the Human Sciences*.

theory itself is inscribed in the expansion of science. To the thinning of the subject through algorithms, psychoanalysis is indeed contributing right now by submitting itself in part to the increasingly rigorous formalization that Lacan demands from its theorization. Let me emphasize two points: first, this formalization is the only way out for theoretical psychoanalysis, lest it be assimilated either to religion or magic; second, and consequently, an obscurantist position that would simply negate the advance of Lacan's "science of the signifier" is not a possibility here.

Lacan's prediction should not be taken lightly by psychoanalysts. They may remember the accuracy of his forecast (at least for France) of the rise of racism in "*Télévision*";[3] the prediction of the demise of psychoanalysis results simply from the direction he has given to theoretical psychoanalysis, a direction in which it can only collaborate to the exhaustion of the subject's singularity.

We may note that no corrective to the impasses of civilization is ever considered, even as a remote possibility, by Lacan; yet pessimism is just as much an imaginary aporia as optimism is; it is up to us to choose our way out of the impasses of civilization.

The apocalypse, however, does have a counterpart for Lacan. This would constitute the moment, at the end of the history of the modern subject (the subject of science), where "the *Ecrits'* indications will be taken up by somebody."

This means that the subject's desire can never be exhausted by its increasing formalization. Indeed, the increasing pressure of science in itself creates unheard-of fantasies, and an increasing desire, due to the dialectics of law and desire. The hope here is that the return of the repressed will be manageable.

Before this historical moment's arrival, we are left, however, with Lacan's immense legacy, which I would characterize as a systematic smashing of all the idols that inhabit our thought. Indeed, I surmise that Lacan, in the history of modern thought, occupies the function of the last destroyer of idols. His contribution, therefore, may be summarized by a series of negative precepts that pertain to the Symbolic order, and are hence real:

---

3. *Autres écrits*, p. 534.

1. There is no whole, because of the Gödelian theorem of incompleteness on the side of science; and on the other side, humanities, because of the existence of an unconscious that resists formalization.
2. There is no wisdom and no serenity, because desire always subverts and outlasts them. Wisdom and serenity presuppose a unified, self-conscious, and therefore masterable subject that does not exist.
3. There is no master, because modern knowledge transmits itself through mathemes, making the presence of the Master's voice unnecessary.
4. There is no soul and no interiority, except as imaginary crutches to defend ourselves against the exteriority of language and the unconscious. Therefore (inasmuch as Aristotle declares the soul the locus of thought), there is no thought, only the materiality of words combined together to support a request or a desire.
5. There are no human sciences, because man is here, at the same time, the subject and the object.
6. There is no other of the Other, and there is no metalanguage: language is the only tool of inquiry at our disposal.
7. And finally: there is no sexual rapport.

All thoughts that contradict these negative propositions belong to the realm of the science of antiquity or are survivals of it. It is possible to summarize this antithesis thus: wholeness, harmony between humankind and the world, and between men and women are not possible. We should note that these ideas are imaginary responses to symbolic constraints. They constitute dreams, fantasies, or illusions, and as such are at the service of life, whereas the death drive, in the form of the human subject's thinning and abolition, is at work in the symbolic precepts. Even if they are not an appropriate response, these ideas are the working fantasies that make life more bearable. That is why these inappropriate "answers" endure and coexist side by side with the symbolic precepts that contradict them. However, even if these illusions dampen our existential malaise, they are tied to mechanisms of repression. They have therefore produced a return of the repressed in the form of scores of irrational responses to the weight of modernity.

That is why Lacan chose the impossible ethics of desire as the only real (i.e., logical) answer to the expansion of science, the increased demands of the superego, the constrictions the symbolic order imposes on modern humanity. It appeared to him to be a rational response to the expansion of rationality itself.

Finally, the purpose of Lacan's work is not to enable us to think better and in a more precise way; after all, we can live perfectly happily with the help of our diverse alienations; our blissful passion for ignorance may even contribute to our happiness. But if we are to address one of the main problems of our time, the progressive abolition of the subject by the expansion of science (or, in Freudian terms, the relentless expansion of the superego), we had better formulate our answers according to a real view of the problem. In a world where, more and more, men and women are aggregated as numbers in sets, it may be high time to consider them one by one, in their singularity. That is the task that Lacan assigned to the treatment by applied psychoanalysis.

Appendix I
The Bar Defined

We have already seen how coherent Lacan's formalizations are: the formula of the sign can be easily inscribed in the schema L, the latter can be transformed into the schema R or a Borromean knot, the schema R can be transformed in a Möbius strip with, at each reinscription, a gain of precision and theoretical understanding. It is not that Lacan was possessed by some prophetic and premonitory spirit, but that the first formalizations, in their accuracy, opened the way for further algorithms borrowed from various domains of mathematics and logic. For example, the vectorial analysis of the schema L, which is already a transformation, opens the way to topological transformations as well as the reinscription of the schema in the Borromean knot, and then the torus can be used to construct a Möbius strip,[1] for example.

The algorithm of the sign is central to the formalization: it is a founding matheme at the root of all previous and subsequent developments. It is also an algorithm that causes hardcore humanists to quit

---

1. See "L'Étourdit," *Autres écrits*, p. 469.

reading Lacan, because mathematical formulation is beyond their understanding, and professional mathematicians to view Lacanian thought as a metaphor without any bearing on their discipline. It is nevertheless possible to give a definition of the bar that will satisfy both mathematical rigor and a layperson's intuition. If the bar cannot be clearly defined, it is no hyperbole to say that the entire edifice of Lacanian theory would collapse. Psychoanalysis then would have to be discarded in the box of traditional Humanities, stuck on the shelf somewhere between religion and magic. Either the algorithms really work, or Lacanian thought is but another reincarnation of the obscurantism of humanism.

A traditional view of the sign reduces it to its signification (its signified representation). It obliterates the symbolic-unconscious part of the sign; it would look something like this:

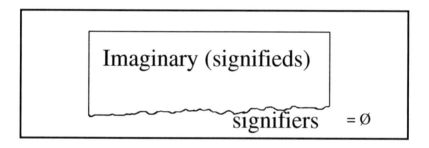

This imaginary representation of the sign reduces it to its represented aspect. Forgotten or repressed is the sign's symbolic-unconscious dimension. This representation stems from humanity's love for its illusions, denials, and fantasies. Its purpose is none other than to maintain the defenses and the repressions of the ego, its fundamental denial of everything unconscious. We can call this one-dimensional representation the neurotic alibi of common sense, whose goal is to consider only the sign's signification, never its true meaning.[2]

---

2. See Chapter 2 of this book, p. 45. This representation is thus related to the University's discourse, as formalized by Lacan. It is a form of "bêtise" (stupidity), if we follow Jean-Claude Milner's developments in *Les noms indistincts* (Paris: Le Seuil, 1983, pp. 132–142).

Another conception (that would be the Derridean or Deleuzian one, and, more generally, the one practiced by academic nominalists in the university) represses the real dimension created by the division of the sign; it derives from a selective (repressive, incomplete) reading of Saussure's *Course in General Linguistics*:[3]

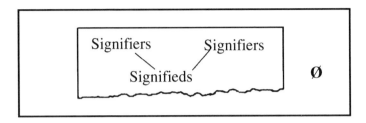

The signifier is reduced to its imaginary dimension, again by a one-dimensional flattening. Hence, nothing real can be affirmed: in the last analysis, a signifier will only refer to another signifier in an infinite regression. It is thus not surprising that deconstruction has nothing to say about science and the real: for this theory, these concepts are nonexistent, they are an empty set. It can be pointed out that this conception has been definitely buried by the scientific revolution, which demonstrates that mathematical signifiers are not just names, but a perfectly adequate description of real processes: the Keplerian ellipsis, for example, *is* a planet's trajectory. The separation of sciences and humanities is further contested by the Lacanian import of logic and mathematics in the Humanities. For example, metaphors and metonymies, these linguistic fictions, respectively *are* the processes of repression and the displacement of desire. In other words, facts and conjectures about something real can be made in the Humanities beyond the self-reflexive wordplay of the signifiers. The flattening of the sign and its assimilation to either signified or signifier leads us down the path of relativism, obscurantism, and a pyrrhonist, generalized doubt. This flattening represents a regression from the logical argument to the principle of authority, where statements are considered true because they are issued by the fathers of philosophy, hence positioned beyond the reach of

---

3. For more details, see pp. 39–40 of this book.

rational argumentation. We can call this second flattening of the sign the Pyrrhonist's psychotic alibi.[4]

This means that our learning institutions, which rigorously separate humanities and sciences, reproduce an outmoded model of knowledge transmission: they are basically the barely modified offspring of the rhetorical model inherited from Antiquity, of the organization of knowledge by the seven liberal arts that has been practiced for at least two millennia. However, our schools are coherent in their misunderstanding of modern knowledge when they separate the developments of Galilean science as a discrete discipline not related to Humanities; our colleges of Arts and Sciences are but a misnomer for Arts *or* Sciences, or even Arts *against* Sciences and vice versa. Suffice to say that our learning institutions should be rebuilt from the ground up; humanists should be taught mathematical reasoning (not too hard a task considering that Lacan's algorithms are fairly basic), and scientists should be made aware of the real existence of the unconscious; but that would be the topic of yet another book.

Let us now discard the flattening of the sign by a definition of the bar. Lacan warns that it cannot be considered a quotient, fraction, or division sign.[5] At the same time, the bar is not a Saussurian barrier; it formalizes the Freudian concept of double inscription by revealing the two sides of any sign: its signifying-unconscious one, and its signified one. The bar can be used according to the rules of algebraic, geometric, or topological mathematics. All these branches of mathematics describe different, but coherent, aspects of the bar.

I will use here topology, since it satisfies mathematicians as well as facilitates an intuitive understanding of the bar. From a one-dimensional representation (supported by the two dimensions of spaces), we jump to a four-dimensional diagram.

The bar, as the cut of interpretation, is ordered by a cross-cap or a Möbius strip.[6] Hence, the bar is none other than the cut that the Möbius strip operates, *it is a Möbius strip* that cuts the sign in its two

---

4. This vision of the sign, in its turn, is closely related to the Master's discourse. Again, see the incisive remarks on "canaillerie" (knavery) by Jean-Claude Milner, *ibid.*, pp. 124–130.

5. See Chapter 2 of this book, pp. 42–43.

6. See "Radiophonie," *Autres écrits*, p. 418.

components and defines them, to produce represented signification and unconscious meaning.[7]

Let us start again from the formula of the sign:

$$\frac{S\{\text{Set of signifiers}\}}{s\{\text{Set of signifieds}\}} = \sigma \text{ (meaning)}$$

This algorithm can be written by using the sets defined by Lacan:

$$\frac{\text{Symbolic order}}{\text{Imaginary order}} = \textbf{Real}$$

Now, let us transform the bar into the one-line border of the Möbius strip, which has only one border. The two sets of the Imaginary and the Symbolic are now discretely defined and so is their relationship. Moreover, the Real, a chaos that resists formalization, emerges to fill in the central void:

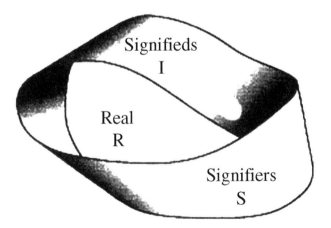

Signifieds
I

Real
R

Signifiers
S

---

7. See "L'Étourdit," *Autres écrits*, pp. 469–470. Regrettably, Lacan didn't illustrate his topological development with the pertinent diagrams. This appendix is meant to partially remedy this lack.

It is therefore possible to construct the Möbian transformation as a proof of the unconscious existence.

The spatial organization of this nonorientable, three-dimensional object is ordered by a fourth dimension, which we can reduce to the time necessary for the sliding on the strip that will at the same time distinguish the signifiers and the signifieds as belonging to two different sets with distinct properties and define their relationship.[8] The temporal sliding of your finger is simply a concrete realization of the geometrical sliding of a vector on the strip. It is the overcoming of the bar, the passage from the signifier to the signified that happens whenever a human being makes a statement. The temporal sliding of the vector or the finger is the reading; it puts into play the human subject in the topological structure. It opens the freedom of an infinite number of readings (of the relationship between signifiers and signifieds). However, this interpretative freedom is at the same time restricted by the Möbius strip's symbolic constraints, which forces us to go in one direction or the other. In the psychoanalytic approach, it is further limited by the impassable obligation of taking into account the real unconscious.

Thus the theory is coherent in all its parts from beginning to end. Reduced to its core components, it is also (I daresay) simple and crystal clear. Lacan's application of mathematical topology to human reality makes him the Einstein of Humanities; it has innumerable consequences and opens up the possibility of an infinite number of research programs.[9]

---

8. Just build a Möbius strip and slide your finger along it. All the concepts developed in Appendix II can of course be inscribed in the different sets defined by the strip.

9. This appendix was written long after the book was completed. It arose from a conversation with Dr. Guissé, to whom I express my deepest gratitude again. It is no exaggeration to say that, without his mathematical insights, this book could not have been written.

Appendix II
Possible Extensions of the Schema L

To summarize in a graphic form the different points made in the book, I present here an extended version of the schema L'; this could be done as easily with the help of the last version of Lacan's topology, the Borromean knot. The power of the graphs can be demonstrated by their capacity to integrate and put into a dialectical relationship as many concepts as possible. What is produced by this integration is the respective positioning of approximate synonyms.

Furthermore, this last graph clearly shows the double inscription of any signifier, one on the stage of "consciousness," and one that Freud called the "other stage" (*die andere Shauplatz*) of the unconscious.[1] For example, a symptom exhibited by a patient will be inscribed as repression as well as repressed.

---

1. See "The Signification of the Phallus," *Ecrits* (English), p. 285.

1. Truth, meaning
2. The mother
3. Real
4. Desire, repressed
5. Drive
6. Impossibility, not-whole, existence
7. Pulverization (sense and nonsense)
8. Femininity, the Thing, the Cause
9. Libido
10. Singularity
11. The analyst
12. God
13. Freud's Id
14. The absence of sexual rapport
15. Limit of speech,
rhetorical figures, and algorithms
16. Applied psychoanalysis

1. Signified, signification
2. The ego and its mirror-image
3. Reality, projections, identifications,
   "consciousness"
4. Request, censorship, sublimation
5. Pleasure
6. Contigence, impotence
7. Consistence
8. Substitute objects (o objects)
9. "Life," love-hate
10. Individuality
11. The University, the Hysteric
12. Belief, faith
13. Freud's ego
14. Imaginary and sexual relationships
15. Combination, metonymy
16. Literary criticism

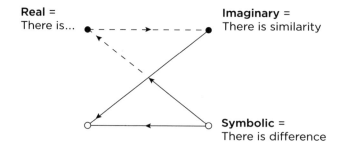

Real =
There is...

Imaginary =
There is similarity

Symbolic =
There is difference

1. Language, signifier
2. The dead father,
   the Name-of-the-Father
3. Fiction
4. Prohibition, repression
5. Jouissance
6. Necessity
7. Differentiation
8. The phallus
9. Death-drive, castration
10. Generality
11. The Master
12. The Church
13. Freud's superego
14. Logical relations, exactitude
15. Substitution, metaphor
16. Theoretical psychoanalysis

Figure A–II. Schema L with approximate synonyms.

Bibliography

1. LACAN (FRENCH)

a. *Séminaires*

Séminaire II, Le moi dans la théorie de Freud et dans la technique de la psychanalyse. Paris: Le Seuil, 1978.
Séminaire III, Les psychoses. Paris: Le Seuil, 1981.
Séminaire VII, Le transfert. Paris: Le Seuil, 1991.
Séminaire VIII, L'éthique de la psychanalyse. Paris: Le Seuil, 1986.
Séminaire XXI, L'identification, unpublished.
Séminaire XI, Les quatre concepts fondamentaux de la psychanalyse. Paris: Le Seuil, 1973.
Séminaire XVII, L'envers de la psychanalyse. Paris: Le Seuil, 1991.
Les non-dupes errent, unpublished seminar, December 11, 1973.
Séminaire XX, Encore! Paris: Le Seuil, 1975.
"Le Séminaire de Caracas," in *L'Âne* 1 (Avril–Mai), 1981.
"Peut-être à Vincennes," *Ornicar?* 1, 1975. See also *Autres écrits*.

"R S I," Ornicar? 2, 4, and 5, 1975–1976.
"Vers un signifiant nouveau," Ornicar? 17–18, 1979.
"Une pratique de bavardage," Ornicar? 19, 1979.

b. Works by Lacan

Écrits. Paris: Le Seuil, 1966.
Autres écrits, ed. Jacques-Alain Miller. Paris: Le Seuil, 2001.
"Discours de clôture du congrès de l'École freudienne sur la transmission," Lettres de l'École freudienne no. 25, 1979. See also Autres écrits.
"Conférences et entretiens dans des universités américaines," Scilicet 6–7, 1976.
"La mort, le rêve, le réveil," transcription by Catherine Millot, L'Âne 3, Automne 1981.
". . . ou pire, Introduction à l'édition allemande d'un premier volume des Écrits," Scilicet 5, 1975. See also Autres écrits.

2. LACAN IN ENGLISH TRANSLATION

Écrits, a Selection, translated by Alan Sheridan. New York: Norton, 1977. New translation by Bruce Fink, New York: Norton, 2002.
"Knowledge and truth," translated by Bruce Fink. Newsletter of the Freudian Field, vol. 3, nos. 1–2, Spring–Fall 1989.
Television, translated by Denis Hollier, Annette Michelson, and Rosalind Krauss. New York: Norton, 1990.
Seminar XX, On Feminine Sexuality, The Limits of Love and Knowledge, translated by Bruce Fink. New York: Norton, 1998.
Seminars I, II, III, VIII, XI, and XX have also been translated and published by Norton.

3. FREUD

Freud, Sigmund. The Ego and the Id. New York: Norton, 1960.
———— Beyond the Pleasure Principle. New York: Norton, 1961.
———— New Introductory Lectures on Psychoanalysis. New York: Norton, 1965.

———— *The Future of an Illusion*. New York: Norton, 1989.

———— *Civilization and Its Discontents*. New York: Norton, 1989.

———— *The Standard Edition of the Complete Psychological Works of Sigmund Freud*, ed. James Strachey. New York: Norton, 1990.

———— *Totem and Taboo*. New York: Norton, 1990.

———— *The Interpretation of Dreams*, *The Basic Writings of Sigmund Freud* (*Psychopathology of Everyday Life, the Interpretation of Dreams, and Three Essays on the Theory of Sexuality*). New York: Basic Books, 2000.

———— *Gesammelte Werke*. Frankfurt: Fischer, 2001.

4. ON LACAN

André, Serge. *What Does a Woman Want?* New York: Other Press, 1999.

Badiou, Alain. "Sujet et infini." In *Conditions*. Paris: Le Seuil, 1992.

Borch-Jacobsen, Mikkel. *Lacan: The Absolute Master*, translated by Douglas Brick. Stanford, CA: Stanford University Press, 1991.

Charraud, Nathalie. *Lacan et les Mathématiques*. Paris: Anthropos, 1997.

Chemama, Roland, and Vandermersch, Bernard, eds. *Dictionnaire de la psychanalyse*. Paris: Larousse, 1998.

Cléro, Jean-Pierre. *Le vocabulaire de Lacan*. Paris: Ellipses, 2002.

Dor, Joël. *Introduction to the Reading of Lacan: The Unconscious Structured Like a Language*. New York: Other Press, 1998.

Feher-Gurewich, Judith, and Tort, Michel. *Lacan and the New Wave in American Psychoanalysis*. New York: Other Press, 1999.

Fink, Bruce. *The Lacanian Subject*. Princeton, NJ: Princeton University Press, 1995.

Goux, Jean-Joseph. "Lacan iconoclast." In *Lacan and the Human Sciences*, ed. Alexandre Leupin. Lincoln, NE: University of Nebraska Press, 1991.

Lee, Jonathan Scott. *Jacques Lacan*. Amherst, MA: University of Massachussetts Press, 1990.

Leupin, Alexandre, ed. *Lacan and the Human Sciences*. Lincoln, NE: University of Nebraska Press, 1991.

Miller, Jacques-Alain, ed. *Qui sont vos psychanalystes?* Paris: Le Seuil, 2002.

Milner, Jean-Claude. *Les noms indistincts*. Paris: Le Seuil, 1983.

———— "Lacan and the ideal of science." In *Lacan and the Human Sciences*, ed. Alexandre Leupin. Lincoln, NE: University of Nebraska Press, 1991.

———— *L'oeuvre claire*. Paris: Le Seuil, 1995.

———— *Le périple structural*. Paris: Le Seuil, 2002.

Mitchell, Juliet, and Rose, Jacqueline. *Feminine Sexuality: Jacques Lacan and the École Freudienne*. New York: Norton, 1982.

Porter, Dennis. "Psychoanalysis and the task of the translator." In *Lacan and the Human Sciences*, ed. Alexandre Leupin. Lincoln, NE: University of Nebraska Press, 1991.

Rabaté, Jean-Michel. *Lacan in America*. New York: Other Press, 2000.

Regnault, François. *Dieu est inconscient*. Paris: Navarin, 1985.

———— "Lacan and experience." In *Lacan and the Human Sciences*, ed. Alexandre Leupin. Lincoln, NE: University of Nebraska Press, 1991.

Roudinesco, Elisabeth. *Histoire de la Psychanalyse en France*. Paris: Le Seuil, 1986. Translated by Jeffrey Mehlman as *Jacques Lacan & Co.: A History of Psychoanalysis in France, 1925–1985*. Chicago: University of Chicago Press, 1990.

———— *Jacques Lacan*. Paris: Fayard, 1993. Translated by Barbara Bray. New York: Columbia University Press, 1997.

Sokal, Alan, and Bricmont, Jean. *Intellectual Impostures: Postmodern Philosophers' Abuse of Science*. London: Profile Books, 1988.

Vanier, Alain. *Lacan*. New York: Other Press, 2002.

Verhaeghe, Paul. *Does the Woman Exist? From Freud's Hysteric to Lacan's Feminine*. New York: Other Press, 1999.

5. OTHER REFERENCES

Aristotle. *De Anima*, Harmondsworth: Penguin Classics, 1987.

———— *Metaphysics*. Harmondsworth: Penguin Classics, 1999.

———— *The Nichomachean Ethics*. Oxford: Clarendon Press, 1999.

Boethius. "Contra Nestorium et Eutychen." In *The Theological Treatises*. Cambridge, MA: Harvard University Press, 1978.

Galileo Galilei. *Dialogue Concerning the Two Chief World Systems*, trans. Stillman Drake. Berkeley: University of California Press, 1962.

Gay, Peter. *Freud, A Life for Our Time.* New York: Norton, 1988.

Kojève, Alexandre. "L'origine chrétienne de la science moderne." In *Mélanges Koyré*, ed. R. Taton and I. Cohen, t. II. Paris: Hermann, 1964.

Kuhn, Thomas S. *The Structure of Scientific Revolutions.* Chicago: University of Chigaco Press, 2nd ed., 1970.

Lakatos, Imre. "Methodology of scientific research programmes." In *Criticism and the Growth of Knowledge*, ed. Imre Lakatos and Alan Musgrave. Cambridge, UK: Cambridge University Press, 1970.

——— "Mathematics science and epistemology." In *Philosophical Papers*, vol. 2. Cambridge, UK: Cambridge University Press, 1978.

Leroi-Gourhan, André. *Treasures of Prehistoric Art.* New York: Abrams, 1980.

Mannoni, Octave. "L'athéisme de Freud." In *Ornicar?* 6:21–32.

Plato. *Meno.* Indianapolis, IN: Hackett, 1980.

Popper, Karl. *Realism and the Aim of Science.* Totowa, NJ: Rowman and Littlefield, 1983.

Saussure, Ferdinand de. *Cours de linguistique générale*, ed. Tullio di Mauro. Paris: Payot, 1972.

Stalin, Joseph V. "Marxism and problems of linguistics." *Pravda*, June 20, July 4, and August 2, 1950.

Starobinski, Jean, ed. *Les mots sous les mots. Les Anagrammes de Ferdinand de Saussure.* Paris: Gallimard, 1971.

Tarski, Alfred. "The semantic conception of truth and the foundations of semantics." *Philosophy and Phenomenological Research* 4 (1944): 341–376.

——— "The concept of truth in formalized languages." In *Logic, Semantics, Metamathematics.* Oxford: Clarendon Press, 1956.

Index